Editor
Brent L. Fox, M. Ed.

Editor in Chief
Karen J. Goldfluss, M.S. Ed.

Creative Director
Sarah M. Fournier

Cover Artist
Diem Pascarella

Art Coordinator
Renée Mc Elwee

Illustrator
Kelly McMahon

Imaging
Amanda R. Harter

Publisher
Mary D. Smith, M.S. Ed.

TCR 3636

INS READING COMPREHENSION PRACTICE

- Provides over 240 fiction and nonfiction quick-read activities for applying eight comprehension strategies

- Reinforces reading skills throughout the year

- Includes a "Strategies in Writing" section to practice comprehension skills in an open-ended, short-answer format

- **Correlated to Common Core State Standards**

Teacher Created Resources

Authors
Ruth Foster, M. Ed.
Mary S. Jones, M. Ed.

CORRELATED TO **COMMON CORE** STANDARDS

For correlations to the Common Core State Standards, see pages 141–142. Correlations can also be found at *http://www.teachercreated.com/standards.*

Teacher Created Resources
6421 Industry Way
Westminster, CA 92683
www.teachercreated.com

ISBN: 978-1-4206-3636-9

© *2015 Teacher Created Resources*
Made in U.S.A.

Teacher Created Resources

Table of Contents

Introduction

Instant Reading Comprehension Practice provides short reading and writing exercises that develop and strengthen the skills needed for reading comprehension.

This book is divided into two main sections: *Comprehension Activities* and *Strategies in Writing*. *Comprehension Activities* is divided into eight sub-sections that focus specifically on each of the following comprehension skills:

- Finding Main Ideas
- Noting Details
- Using Context Clues
- Identifying Facts and Opinions
- Finding Cause and Effect
- Sequencing
- Making Inferences
- Predicting Outcomes

Each sub-section includes at least 30 passages with questions designed to challenge students and guide them towards mastery in one of the eight skill areas.

The *Strategies in Writing* section provides students with the opportunity to identify and practice the same comprehension skills but in an open-ended, short-answer format. The activities in this section allow students to focus on a specific strategy and to think more critically as they respond to a given writing task.

How to Use This Book

A teacher can

- choose to focus on one skill exclusively, going sequentially through the exercises.

- do a few exercises from each skill set to provide daily variety.

- assign specific exercises that will introduce, match, and/or strengthen strategies covered in the classroom.

Writing activities can be assigned at any time and in any order, but each activity focuses on a particular strategy. The strategy is noted at the top of the page. Each strategy has four activity pages, except for *Making Inferences* and *Predicting Outcomes*, which have three each.

Teaching Tips for Specific Exercises

You may want to go through one or two exercises together with the class.

At first, focus on critical-thinking skills rather than speed. Fluency and rate of reading will improve as students practice and gain confidence with each targeted skill.

Remind students that they should read EVERY answer choice. The first answer may sound correct, but there might be a better choice. If they can cross out just one wrong answer, they will have a much better chance of choosing the correct answer.

Finding Main Ideas

Students may find it helpful to sum up what they just read in a short sentence or two before reading the answer choices. Other students may find it helpful to first make a list of three or four key words from the text. Both strategies can help students focus on the most important parts of a passage and not be mislead by incorrect answer choices.

Remind students to choose an answer that covers most of whom or what the paragraph is about. Usually, wrong answers will focus either on details that are too small or too broad. For example, in a paragraph about what bats eat, how they are the only flying mammals, and how they raise their babies, an answer that *only* talks about what bats eat is too "small." An answer that talks about *all* kinds of mammals is too "big." The main idea is bats, not mammals like bears, lions, and porcupines! In other words, students should be thinking, "Not too big, not too small, but just right!"

Pick the correct answer. Students should think about what answer is too big, too small, just right . . . or just wrong!

You let a thirsty camel drink. The camel has not had water for one week. It has not eaten for a month. Its hump is leaning over and drooping. How much water can the camel drink? It can drink up to 32 gallons!

What is the main idea?

A. All animals need water to survive. (too big)

B. The camel has a drooping hump. (too small)

C. A thirsty camel can drink up to 32 gallons of water. (just right)

Noting Details

Remind students not to panic if they read a passage with a lot of details. They do not have to memorize or remember all the facts and figures! They can always go back and check the passage. Read the following example:

> Most of Earth is covered by oceans. The largest ocean is the Pacific Ocean. The second-largest ocean is the Atlantic Ocean. The third-largest ocean is the Indian Ocean.
>
> What is the second-largest ocean?
>   A. the Pacific Ocean
>   B. the Atlantic Ocean
>   C. the Indian Ocean   *Answer: B*

Ask students if they had to memorize what they read to answer the question or if they went back and looked it up. Point out that all the information they need is still right in front of them and can be reread as many times as necessary.

Using Context Clues

Remind students not to stop reading! Reassure students that they are not expected to know what a word means or what word should go in the blank. They are solving a puzzle! They **must** finish reading the prompt. Then, they can reread the sentence while inserting one of the answer choices into the blank. Usually, they can eliminate choices because some answers will not make sense.

For example, no one expects a child to know the word *defenestrate* (to throw a thing or oneself out of a window). Yet students can correctly choose it if they use the process of elimination, as seen in the following example:

> The firefighter had to _____ himself onto a big air pillow when he could not go down the stairs.
>
> What word best completes the sentence?
>   A. sweep
>   B. defenestrate
>   C. bike   *Answer: B*

Point out that even if they couldn't read the word *defenestrate*, they could cross out and eliminate *sweep* and *bike*. They could still get the right answer!

Identifying Facts and Opinions

Have students ask themselves, "Is this something I think, or do I know for certain?"

> *Blue flowers are better than orange flowers.* If I **think** it, it is an **opinion**.

> *Some plants have flowers.* If it is **certain** or if I can **prove** it, then it is a **fact**.

Finding Cause and Effect

Have students ask themselves, "What happened, and why did it happen?"

What happened is the **effect**. **Why** it happened is the **cause**. If they forget this, students can write **What** = **Effect** and **Why** = **Cause** on the top of their page until the information can easily be recalled.

Example: When Sam read the book, he learned that a hippo has a two-foot wide lip!

What happened? (**effect**) Sam learned something. Why did it happen? (**cause**) Sam read a book.

Sequencing

Ask students to read over the sentences in the order students think the sentences happened. Think about what comes first and what comes later. Think about whether the order makes sense. Make sure the last sentence could not have happened until the previous ones did. Consider the following example:

> **1.** Sally started sneezing.
>
> **2.** Sally found a pretty flower on her way to school.
>
> **3.** She picked the flower and smelled it.
>
> What is the correct sequence?
> **A.** 1, 2, 3
> **B.** 3, 2, 1
> **C.** 2, 3, 1
> *Answer: C*

Making Inferences

When we make an inference, we use **clues** from the story to figure out something the author hasn't told us.

Example: Caesar's heart pounded! He felt a cold trickle of sweat run down his back.

Most likely, was Caesar hungry, tired, or afraid? If Caesar was hungry, it is doubtful that he would be having such a strong physiological reaction. The same logic can be applied to being tired. Being afraid is the only logical answer.

Predicting Outcomes

When we predict an outcome, we make a logical guess about what is going to happen next. Remind students not to answer what happened. They should only be concerned about what might happen in the **future**.

Example: The air was filled with mosquitoes. Lizzie went outside in shorts and a sleeveless shirt.

Have students make logical guesses about what might happen next. (Lizzie gets bitten; she puts on different clothes; she puts on insect repellent, etc.)

Remember: Insist that students read every answer choice! Have them eliminate or cross out the answer choices that don't make sense or that they know are wrong!

Name _____ Date _____

Snowy Surprise

A polar bear sometimes covers its nose and mouth with its paw. It does this when it is hunting. A polar bear does not want to be seen. It wants to surprise its prey. It covers its dark nose and mouth so it cannot be seen. This makes the bear hard to see in its white, snowy world.

What is the main idea?

 A. A polar bear covers its nose and mouth while hunting in order to blend in with the snow.
 B. A polar bear covers its nose and mouth to hide from other bears.
 C. A polar bear sometimes covers its nose and mouth after a big meal.

Dizzy Days

The carnival ride went around and around. Michael did not feel very well. He thought he was going to be sick if he did not get off the ride soon. Finally, the ride stopped. He was glad the spinning ride was over. Now he just wished the ground would stop spinning!

What is the main idea?

 A. Michael went on a spinning carnival ride that made him very dizzy.
 B. Michael got very sick after the spinning ride was over.
 C. Michael saw the ground spinning after he spun himself around in circles.

Name _____ Date _____

A Hole in One

Morgan and three of her friends played miniature golf after school. At Hole 9, Morgan went first. She had to hit her ball over a bridge and through a tunnel. The ball would come out on the other side. Morgan firmly swung her club. The ball went straight, just missing the edge of the bridge. Morgan didn't see her ball on the other side. Her friend found it, though. Morgan had made a hole in one!

What is the main idea?

A. Morgan liked playing miniature golf with her friends.
B. Morgan could not find her ball on the other side of the tunnel.
C. Morgan hit her ball over the bridge and made a hole in one.

Lost Friend

After looking for three hours, Robert and Wade could not find their dog, Rover. They knew Rover could not have gone far. Rover had a hurt leg. The boys made signs and put Rover's picture on each one. They wrote, "Call if you find our missing dog." They hung the signs all around the neighborhood. The next day, they got an important phone call. Rover was found!

LOST!

ROVER
CALL IF YOU FIND
OUR MISSING DOG.
(562) 555-1468

What is the main idea?

A. Someone in the neighborhood found Rover after three hours.
B. Robert and Wade used signs to find their missing dog, Rover.
C. Rover hurt his leg and could not go far.

Name _____ **Date** _____

Big Cats

The serval is a cat. It is a wild cat. It lives in Africa. A serval can weigh up to 40 pounds. A lion is wild cat. It lives in Africa, too. A lion can weigh 400 pounds. The serval is smaller, but one thing is bigger—its ears! No other cat has ears as big as a serval's. If a serval had your size head, its ears would be as big as a dinner plate!

What is the main idea?

  A. Many wild cats live in Africa.
  B. Servals have the largest ears of any cat.
  C. Lions weigh a lot more than servals.

Shoe Business

Emily needed new shoes—again. All of her shoes were too small. Her father took her to the shoe store. "We're looking for size 2 shoes," he said to the clerk. Emily tried on three pairs of sneakers. She picked one that fit just right. When they got home, she noticed there were two pairs in the bag. "That one's a size 3 to save us a trip to the shoe store next month," said her father with a smile.

What is the main idea?

  A. Emily had to try on three pairs of shoes until she found one that fit just right.
  B. Emily wanted size 2 shoes because she didn't like the way her shoes looked.
  C. Emily's dad bought her extra shoes because all of her shoes were too small.

Name _____ **Date** _____

Speedy Sneezys

When you sneeze, air rushes out of your nose and mouth. The air can rush out as fast as a car speeding down the road. All sneezes send out tiny particles. When sick people sneeze, their germs can spread through the air. Always cover your mouth and nose with a tissue when you sneeze. Don't forget to wash your hands!

What is the main idea?

  A. It is important to cover your mouth and nose with a tissue when you sneeze.
  B. A sneeze and a car can travel at the same speed.
  C. Sick people sneeze more often than healthy people.

Fright Night!

It was very dark! Anthony needed a flashlight from the hall. By habit, he reached for the hall light switch. Of course, it didn't work. Anthony crept down the hall. He felt as though he was trapped deep inside a cave. Why did the power have to fail during a nighttime thunderstorm? This wouldn't be so scary in the daytime.

What is the main idea?

  A. The batteries in Anthony's flashlight died one night.
  B. Anthony was afraid when the power went out one night during a storm.
  C. Anthony enjoys pretending he's trapped inside a cave in the dark.

Name _____ Date _____

Danger Drop

The Danger Drop was the scariest, fastest waterslide at the water park. Kimiko had always wanted to try it. Each time she went to the park, she got in line to ride it. When she reached the front of the line, she got out. She was just too scared. One day when it was her turn, she sat down, closed her eyes, and went down the Danger Drop. Kimiko had so much fun. She couldn't wait to go on it again.

What is the main idea?

  A. Kimiko never got over her fear of going on the Danger Drop.
  B. Kimiko was sure that she would never go on the Danger Drop again.
  C. Kimiko got over her fear of the Danger Drop after she went down it.

The Human Spider

Alain Robert has a nickname. Alain's nickname is "The Human Spider." Alain climbs skyscrapers. Alain does not use a ladder. He doesn't use a rope. He only uses two things. He uses climbing shoes. He uses a bag of chalk powder. Alain rubs the chalk on his hands to keep them from slipping.

What is the main idea?

  A. Climbers use chalk to keep from slipping.
  B. Spiders have nicknames.
  C. Alain Robert climbs skyscrapers.

Name _____ Date _____

Four-Legged Friend

My cat Socks followed me everywhere I went. When I dug in the sandbox, Socks dug too. When I played on the grass, can you guess who played with me? One day, I was watering the plants. Socks followed me. Socks thought he could catch the water. Socks did not expect to get wet! Now Socks doesn't follow me around anymore.

What is the main idea?

A. Socks follows his owner around, no matter what.
B. Socks doesn't follow his owner anymore because he doesn't like getting wet.
C. Socks doesn't follow his owner because he would rather dig in the sand.

Race to the Finish

The race was about to start. Carla, Amber, Kate, and Kenesha were at the starting line. "On your mark. Get set. Go!" shouted Jane. Around the track they went. The four friends were close together most of the way. Kate started falling behind. Kenesha tripped over a rock and fell. Amber took the lead and crossed the finish line first.

What is the main idea?

A. Four friends ran a race, and Amber won.
B. The four friends were tied most of the way until Carla tripped.
C. Jane yelled "Go!" so the race could begin.

Name _____ **Date** _____

A Fish Tale

Quickly, Tim started to reel in his line. The fish tugged and pulled hard. Judging by the weight of his catch, Tim thought this fish could feed his family for two days. Tim struggled to stay in the boat and not be pulled over the side. Finally, his catch came into view. He had snagged a snapping turtle.

What is the main idea?

A. Tim met his goal of catching a snapping turtle.

B. Tim caught a fish big enough to feed his family for two days.

C. Tim thought he had caught a big fish, but it turned out to be a snapping turtle.

First-Day Fashion

The new school year was about to start. Addie wanted to get new clothes. While shopping with her mom, Addie found a nice outfit. "This will be perfect for the first day of school," she said. The next morning, Addie walked into her new class. She saw her best friend Mara wearing the exact same outfit that she had on. "Great minds think alike," Addie said.

What is the main idea?

A. Addie was upset that Mara was wearing the same outfit on the first day of school.

B. Addie and Mara both wore the same outfit on the first day of school.

C. Addie and Mara planned to dress the same on the first day of school.

The Picky Parrot

George got a pet parrot for his birthday. He wanted to teach his parrot to talk. He tried to get his bird to say, "Birdie wants a cracker," but Birdie would not say it. One day, George was eating a cookie. He heard, "Birdie wants a cookie." George could not believe it. Birdie could talk! He just didn't like crackers.

What is the main idea?

   A. George's pet parrot does not like crackers.
   B. George's pet parrot wouldn't talk for crackers, but it talked for cookies.
   C. George's pet parrot talks every time George is eating a food that it wants.

Across the Ice

Ann Bancroft is an explorer. Ann and another explorer went to Antarctica. They skied across the ice. Ann pulled a sled while she skied. Ann's sled was very heavy. It weighed 250 pounds!

What is the main idea?

   A. Ann's sled weighed 250 pounds.
   B. An explorer skied across Antarctica.
   C. Ann does not like to ski down hills.

Name _____ **Date** _____

Jumping for Joy

Jackson wished he had a trampoline at home so he could jump and jump. Jackson's family lived in an apartment, so there was no yard for a trampoline. One day, Jackson's dad parked the car in front of a tall building. "Where are we?" Jackson asked his dad. Jackson's dad said, "This is a place where kids can play on indoor trampolines. You can jump all day!"

What is the main idea?

A. Jackson can't jump on a trampoline at home because it is too noisy.

B. Jackson's apartment doesn't have a trampoline, so his dad lets him jump on his bed.

C. Jackson can't jump on a trampoline at home, so his dad took him to a place where kids can jump on trampolines for fun.

A Star Is Born

Everyone was surprised when shy little Beth stepped out onto the stage during the school talent show. She sang a song that she had written herself. No one knew Beth could sing so well! When the song was over, the crowd clapped. Beth smiled and took a bow. Beth decided she wouldn't feel so shy the next time.

What is the main idea?

A. Beth sang a song she had written for the school talent show.

B. Beth felt shy when people clapped.

C. No one could believe that Beth could write a song.

Name _____   Date _____

What a Knight!

Sir Silly was the newest knight in the village. Although he tried his best, he just barely passed his knight training. During his first joust class, he held his lance backwards. During sword class, he swung his sword like a golf club. But Sir Silly never gave up. He finally learned how to be a true knight.

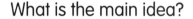

What is the main idea?

A. Sir Silly's knight training didn't go well at first, but by the end, he learned how to be a knight.

B. Sir Silly tried his best to be the funniest knight in the village.

C. Sir Silly didn't pass his knight training because he kept doing silly things.

A Huge Heart

Lots of animals can look in windows. One animal can look in a window on the second floor! The animal can because it is tall. It has long legs. It has a neck as long as its legs. The animal is the tallest land animal. The animal is the giraffe! Your heart is about the size of your fist. A giraffe's heart is big. It is about two feet long. It weighs about 25 pounds.

What is the main idea?

A. A giraffe's neck is as long as its legs.

B. Many animals like to look in windows.

C. The giraffe is the tallest land animal.

Name _____ Date _____

Birthday Surprise

Paul and his mom share the same birthday. Paul's aunt gave him a $30 gift card to his favorite store as an early birthday present. "Now I can buy the DVD that I want," he said. When Paul went to that store, they were all out of the DVD he wanted. So Paul thought of a different idea. He ended up using the gift card to buy his mom a new pair of shoes for her birthday. Paul's mom loved her new shoes. Paul was happy with his purchase.

What is the main idea?

A. Paul used his birthday gift card to buy something for his mom instead of for himself.
B. Paul used his gift card to buy his mom's present on Mother's Day.
C. Paul wanted to buy a DVD, but he bought himself shoes instead.

Big Bones

The femur, or thigh bone, is the largest bone in the body. It is also the strongest. The femur supports much of the body's weight. This bone extends from the hip joint down to the knee joint. Many people have broken a bone. Most likely, it wasn't the femur. The femur is such a strong bone that it takes a very strong force to break it.

What is the main idea?

A. The femur extends from the hip joint down to the knee joint.
B. The femur is the largest and strongest bone in the body.
C. Many people have broken a bone in their body.

Name _____ Date _____

Nature's Medicine

Aloe vera gel is a natural product that helps heal and soothe the skin. An aloe vera plant has thick leaves. Its leaves are full of sap that looks and feels like jelly. This sap is used to make aloe gel. Many people use it like lotion to help heal sunburns. When they rub it on their skin, the burn gets cooled off.

What is the main idea?

A. Aloe vera gel is a natural product that helps heal and soothe the skin.
B. Many people use aloe vera gel-like lotion to help heal sunburns.
C. An aloe vera plant has thick leaves that are full of sap.

Goodbye, Green

Jan's favorite color is green. Her closet is full of green clothes. Jan even does her homework with a green pen. It drives Jan's teacher crazy when she sees Jan's green-ink homework! Jan's teacher wants Jan to enjoy learning, so she lets Jan use green ink. One night, Jan's green pen ran out of ink. It was too late to go buy a new one. Jan did what her teacher always suggested she do. Jan used a pencil!

What is the main idea?

A. Jan writes with green ink to drive her teacher crazy.
B. Jan won't do her homework if she can't write with green ink.
C. Even though Jan likes writing in green, she used a pencil when her pen ran out of ink.

Name _____ Date _____

Baby Talk

Baby animals have special names. There are lots of different baby animal names. A baby bear is called a cub. A baby bird is called a chick. A baby deer is called a fawn. Some young animals' names depend on whether they are males or females. A young male horse is called a colt. A young female horse is called a filly.

What is the main idea?

A. A baby bird is called a chick.
B. Baby animals have special names.
C. A young horse is either a colt or a filly.

A Full Deck

A normal deck of playing cards has fifty-two cards in it. There are four each of the numbers 2 through 10, along with four jacks, queens, kings, and aces. Each set of thirteen cards has its own suit, or symbol. The suits are hearts, diamonds, spades, and clubs. The spade symbol looks like a shovel. The club symbol looks like a three-leaf clover. Hearts and diamonds are red. Spades and clubs are black.

What is the main idea?

A. There are 13 playing cards in every suit.
B. A deck of playing cards has 52 cards and four suits.
C. Hearts and diamond cards are red; spades and clubs are black.

FINDING MAIN IDEAS: Comprehension Activities

Name _____ Date _____

Doggy Decisions

It was a hot day at the beach. Leo and his sister Rose were playing by the water with their dog, Rex. Every time they threw a stick, Rex would go get it. After some time, Rex was tired. Just as Rose was about to throw the stick, Rex pulled it out of her hand and quickly buried it in the sand. "I guess he's done playing fetch," said Leo.

What is the main idea?

A. Rex fetched the stick until Leo and Rose stopped throwing it for him.
B. Rex fetched the stick until Leo told him to bury it in the sand.
C. Rex fetched the stick over and over until he was too tired.

The Boy Who Could (Almost) Fly

The wind was blowing so hard it made the kite hard to control. Pablo felt as though he was going to fly away! His hands were getting tired of holding on to the string handle. Little by little, he wound the string back onto the handle. Finally, the kite was safe on the ground. Pablo was glad he was, too.

What is the main idea?

A. Pablo had a hard time controlling his kite on a very windy day.
B. It was so windy that Pablo's kite handle flew right out of his hands.
C. While flying a kite on a very windy day, Pablo got tired and needed to rest.

©Teacher Created Resources   19   #3636 Instant Reading Comprehension Practice

Name _____ **Date** _____

A Surprise Visitor

Cara and Matt were looking for shells on the beach. They wanted to start a collection. Cara found one and showed it to Matt. Suddenly, Cara felt the shell move in her hand! Inside the shell was a small sea creature. The shell was its home. Cara decided to put the animal back in the water. Cara and Matt watched the animal until it was gone from their sight.

What is the main idea?

A. Cara put a shell back when she found out it had a live sea animal inside it.

B. Matt wanted to keep the live sea animal in the shell that Cara had found.

C. Matt and Cara started a shell collection.

The Riddle

Sarah told Jonathon that she was thinking of something. She said she didn't think Jonathon could guess what it was. She said it was as light as a feather. It was light, but no one could hold it very long. Even a strong man or woman could not hold it for long. When Sarah stopped talking, Jonathon was quiet. He thought about what Sarah said. Then he said, "I know what you are thinking of! You are thinking of your breath!"

What is the main idea?

A. Sarah knew what strong men and women could do.

B. Sarah had something that was light as a feather.

C. Sarah played a guessing game with Jonathon.

Name _____   **Date** _____

Summer Fun

Doug and Jeff played a game. They tossed a water balloon back and forth to each other. Doug tossed the water balloon to Jeff, but Jeff missed it. It popped on the ground. Doug got another water balloon.

Where did the water balloon pop?

A. in Jeff's hands

B. on the ground

C. on Doug's shoe

Feeding Frenzy

Perry Park has a large water area filled with ducks. People always go to that park to feed the ducks. They bring bread and throw little pieces of it. The ducks race to get as many pieces as they can.

Which park has ducks?

A. Polly Park

B. Patty Park

C. Perry Park

Name _____   **Date** _____

Everybody Dance!

Jenny and Carla are in the same dance class. They will both dance in Friday's show. Jenny and her partner will dance to a fast song. Carla and her partner will dance to a slow song. Everyone will do a few group dances.

Who will dance to a fast song?

A. Jenny and Carla

B. Jenny and her partner

C. Carla and her partner

Loud Laundry

A weird noise was coming from Victor's bedroom. Victor walked all around the room. He wanted to know what the weird noise was. Victor lifted up a shirt that was on the floor. Then he found his toy robot that had been left on.

Where was the noise coming from?

A. from Victor's toy

B. from Victor's backpack

C. from Victor's phone

Name _____ **Date** _____

Fishing with Dad

Suzu and her dad went fishing at their local lake. They set up their gear on the dock. Suzu got to bait the hook and cast the line. After four minutes, her fishing pole began to bend. Suzu had caught her first fish!

Who was Suzu with?

   A. Suzu was with her brother.
   B. Suzu was with her dad.
   C. Suzu was by herself.

A Rough Start

Richard was running late for school. He grabbed his backpack and hopped onto his bike. Richard pedaled as fast as he could. He locked up his bike and ran to his class just before the bell rang.

How did Richard get to school?

   A. He rode his bike.
   B. He ran.
   C. He walked.

Name _____ **Date** _____

Rebecca and the Bear

Rebecca was a firefighter. During one fire, Rebecca had to make a fire break. She cleared trees and brush in the forest. She made a line where the ground was bare. There was nothing for the fire to burn. Then Rebecca saw a bear! Rebecca said, "The bear can go across the bare ground, but the fire cannot!"

Where does Rebecca work?

A. She works in the city.

B. She works in the zoo.

C. She works in the forest.

Animal Artist

Garret likes to paint pictures of animals. He has an art easel in his living room. It has a large sheet under it in case he drips any paint. Garret puts his paintings outside to dry. Then he hangs them all up in his bedroom.

Where does Garret hang up his paintings?

A. outside

B. in his bedroom

C. in the living room

Name _____ Date _____

Pants Problem

Tony's aunt got him a sweater and a pair of pants for his birthday. The sweater fit him just right. The pants were very long on him. Tony's mother asked Tony's aunt where she got the pants. Then Tony's mother took the pants back to the store. She traded the pants for a shorter pair.

What did Tony get from his aunt?

A. a sweater and pants
B. a sweater and a T-shirt
C. a T-shirt and pants

Up to Date

On New Year's Day, Wendy bought a new calendar. The first thing she wrote on it was all the days that her school is closed. Then she wrote all of her friends' birthdays. She hung up the new calendar in her bedroom.

When did Wendy buy a new calendar?

A. while in New York
B. on New Year's Eve
C. on New Year's Day

Name _____ **Date** _____

Meeting Patch

Marcy was very surprised when her mother brought home a new kitten. It was gray with white patches. "Let's name it Patch," said Marcy. Marcy was so happy to have a pet kitten. She played chase with Patch all day.

Who is Patch?

  A. Marcy's mom
  B. Marcy's friend
  C. Marcy's kitten

No More Fears

Gabe likes to go snow-skiing in the winter. When Gabe was learning to ski, he was afraid of falling. Now Gabe skis very well. He is not afraid anymore.

When does Gabe go skiing?

  A. in the summer
  B. in the spring
  C. in the winter

Name _____ Date _____

Treasure in the Park

Kim's friends drew a treasure map for her to follow. They buried a prize for her at the park. The map said to start at the picnic tables. Kim followed the map directions until she got to the place where "X marked the spot." She dug in the dirt and found a bag of coins.

Where was the prize buried?

A. in dirt at the park

B. under the picnic tables

C. in sand at the park

Wheels and Meals

Spencer had a new neighbor named Chen. Spencer and Chen rode to the park. There, they rode around the pond until lunchtime. At lunchtime, they rode to Spencer's house to make sandwiches. First, the boys took out bread. Next, they took out ham and cheese. Then, they took out lettuce and tomato.

Where did the boys make the sandwiches?

A. at the park

B. at Spencer's house

C. at Chen's house

27

Name _____ **Date** _____

Puppy Pals

Leo and Max are puppies. Cooper got them from his mom for his eighth birthday. Leo and Max run and play all day. Leo and Max have a lot of energy! Cooper likes taking care of them. Giving them a bath is his favorite thing to do.

Who gives the puppies a bath?

A. Cooper

B. Cooper's mom

C. nobody

Camp Living Room

The four Smith sisters were pretending to camp in their living room. Susan and Sally moved the furniture to make room for the tent. Summer and Sophie set up the tent. The sisters stayed up late telling stories in the tent.

Who set up the tent?

A. Sharon and Summer

B. Sophie and Sally

C. Sophie and Summer

28

Quackers and Water

Christy has a duck named Quackers. Christy wanted to give Quackers a bath. Christy filled up a large, metal bucket with water. Then she picked up Quackers and tried to put him in the water. Quackers jumped out of Christy's hands. Then Quackers went swimming in the pool behind the barn.

Where did Christy try to bathe Quackers?

A. in a large bucket
B. in a bathtub
C. in a swimming pool

Going, Going, Gone

Yoshi, Sam, and Ethan were playing baseball in their back yard. Yoshi pitched the ball to Ethan. Ethan hit the ball hard, and the ball went over the fence. Sam and Ethan walked to the neighbor's house together and asked for their ball back.

Where did the ball go?

A. through a window
B. into the bushes
C. over the fence

Name _____ **Date** _____

Say, "Cheese!"

Today is "picture day" at school. Jamie chose a pretty green dress to wear. Her mom helped her style her hair. Jamie's class took pictures right before lunch. Jamie is excited to see how her picture turns out.

When did Jamie get her picture taken?

    A. right after lunch

    B. right before lunch

    C. right before recess

Flag Gab

Chase, Eric, and Juan were talking about flags. Chase liked the California state flag best. He liked the bear on it. The state flag of Alaska has stars on it. Eric liked that flag best. Juan liked Wyoming's flag. He liked it because it has a buffalo on it.

Which state flag has a bear on it?

    A. the state flag that Chase liked

    B. the Wyoming state flag

    C. the state flag that Eric liked

Name _____ **Date** _____

Smiles After the Storm

Megan and Kareem saw a rainbow. Megan said her favorite color was green. Kareem said he liked blue the best. Their mom took a picture of them with the rainbow in the background.

Who liked green the best?

A. Kareem

B. Megan

C. their mom

Pony Promises

Ruth has wanted a pony for a long time. Ruth and her parents have talked about how to care for a pony. Ruth must feed it, water it, and clean up after it. Ruth must ride it, too. On her birthday, Ruth was very happy to get a pony from her parents.

What did Ruth and her parents have talks about?

A. what kind of pony to get

B. what to name their pony

C. how to care for a pony

Name _____ **Date** _____

The Lonely Walk

Jake lives one mile away from school. He and his neighbor, Zach, walk together every school day. On Tuesday, Jake walked to school by himself. Zach was not feeling well that day.

When did Jake walk by himself?

A. on Monday
B. on Tuesday
C. on Thursday

Bookworm

Lucy likes to read a lot of books. She likes to read books about animals. She likes to read about princesses, too. One time, Lucy read a book about a red fox. Another time, she read a book about a snow princess. Lucy has two books with blue covers. One book is about a green frog. The other book is about a princess and a dragon.

Which book has a blue cover?

A. the book about the green frog
B. the book about the red fox
C. the book about the snow princess

Name _____   **Date** _____

A Surprising Discovery

Jasmine was swimming. She wore a mask on her face so she could look at fish under the water. Jasmine saw something. It was an eye! It was the size of a half-dollar. It was staring up at her! Jasmine had found a giant oarfish. Giant oarfish are very rare. Few people have seen one. Jasmine's oarfish was 18 feet long!

What is true about the oarfish?

A. Its face was 18 feet long.
B. It was found on the shore.
C. Its eye was the size of a half-dollar.

Being Crafty

Deven and Ben went to the craft store last week. They needed to buy different colors of string for their school project. The store clerk helped them find the string they needed. The boys bought red, yellow, and blue string.

When did the boys go to the craft store?

A. yesterday
B. last week
C. last month

Name _____ Date _____

Sack Race

Ray, Jay, May, and Kay each stepped into an empty potato sack. When Carrie blew the whistle, they all started hopping as fast as they could. Jay and Kay crossed the finish line at the same time. They tied for first place.

Who got first place?

A. Kay and Jay

B. Ray and May

C. Jay

Laundry Day

Donna and her brother David like to work as a team to do chores. They do laundry every Friday. Donna gets the clothes started in the washer. David moves all the clothes to the dryer. They both fold the clothes and put them away.

When do Donna and David do laundry?

A. every Monday

B. every Friday

C. every Thursday

34

Name _____ **Date** _____

Olympic Dreams

Daniel likes running. He likes sprinting, and he likes running long distances. He always asks his friends to race him on the track at school. Daniel would like to compete in the Olympic Games one day. Daniel runs five times a week to practice.

How often does Daniel run?

   A. three times a week
   B. four times a week
   C. five times a week

Lots-o-Legs

Skippy said, "I am glad I am not an ant. Ants are insects. Insects have three body parts, but they only have six legs." Skippy did not have three body parts. He only had two, but he had more than six legs. Skippy had eight legs because he was a spider.

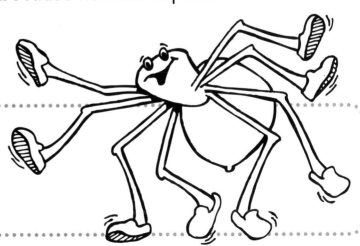

Why is an ant an insect?

   A. It has six legs.
   B. It has two body parts.
   C. It has eight legs.

Name _____ **Date** _____

Riding High

Last week, Bob _____ a horse for the first time. He felt as though he was very high off the ground.

Which word best completes the sentence?

A. road

B. painted

C. rode

A Summer Treat

Lim Sing's ice cream _____ while she was eating it on a hot, summer day.

Which word best completes the sentence?

A. hardened

B. froze

C. melted

Name _____ Date _____

Cheap Seats

To get a better view of the show, Jayden _____ his chair to the left.

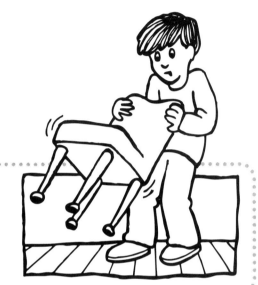

Which word best completes the sentence?

A. broke

B. turned

C. colored

Missed Call

Marta didn't answer her phone when her mom called. Her mom left a _____ telling Marta to call her back.

Which word best completes the sentence?

A. message

B. present

C. story

Name _____ **Date** _____

A Happy Helper

Logan enjoys helping out at the library on weekends. He _____ twice a month.

Which word best completes the sentence?

   A. volunteers

   B. sings

   C. catches

Breakfast Time!

Ava had a _____ to make. She needed to choose either waffles or pancakes for breakfast.

Which word best completes the sentence?

   A. project

   B. decision

   C. trouble

Name _____ **Date** _____

A New Type of Sandwich

Mason saw a funny sandwich. The cheese was on top of two slices of bread. The cheese was not _____ the bread slices.

Which word best completes the sentence?

 A. begin
 B. because
 C. between

Who's Right?

Riley thinks soccer is the best sport. Olivia has a different _____. She thinks basketball is the best sport.

Which word best completes the sentence?

 A. friend
 B. opinion
 C. project

Name _____ **Date** _____

Shake, Rattle, and Roll

The earthquake made everything shake. It even made my
knees _____!

Which word best completes the sentence?

   A. tremble

   B. grow

   C. laugh

Grocery-Store Guy

Jacob walked _____ the store. He went up and down every
aisle. He looked for all the things on his list.

Which word best completes the sentence?

   A. through

   B. threw

   C. under

Name _____ **Date** _____

Early Explorers

The Spanish sailors took their ship on a long _____. They went all the way across the Atlantic Ocean.

Which word best completes the sentence?
- **A.** accident
- **B.** voyage
- **C.** party

A Long Walk Home

Keiko's car stopped working when it ran out of <u>fuel</u>. She needed to buy more from the gas station.

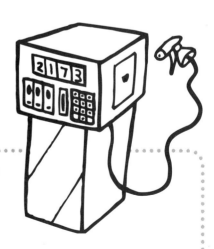

Which word can best replace the underlined word?
- **A.** chips
- **B.** gas
- **C.** milk

Name _____ Date _____

Gold in the Ground

The gold miner could not believe his eyes. He had found gold! After all his hard work, he was now going to be a very <u>wealthy</u> man.

Which word can best replace the underlined word?

A. curious

B. sleepy

C. rich

Off Her Feet

The doctor told Grandma to <u>elevate</u> her feet all day. He said she should place her feet on top of three pillows.

Which word can best replace the underlined word?

A. wash

B. lower

C. raise

Name _____ **Date** _____

Surrounded by Stripes

Henry painted stripes on the wall. Henry made <u>vertical</u> stripes. One end of the stripes touched the floor. The other end of the stripes touched the ceiling.

The underlined word means

  A. side to side.
  B. straight up and down.
  C. round.

Two Toys in One

Leon's new toy can <u>transform</u> into different shapes. It can look like a car. Then, with a push of a button, it can turn into a robot.

The underlined word means

  A. change.
  B. stay the same.
  C. roll away.

Name _____   Date _____

Map Reading

The map <u>legend</u> shows that a star on the map means there is a capital city. A blue line on the map means there is a river.

Which word can best replace the underlined word?

- **A.** street
- **B.** key
- **C.** chair

Practicing for the Game

Emma went to the basketball court. She <u>attempted</u> to make ten baskets, but she only made six.

Which word can best replace the underlined word?

- **A.** lied
- **B.** stretched
- **C.** tried

Name _____ **Date** _____

Don't Be a Litterbug

"You should always put your trash into the trash can," Dana said. "You should not <u>discard</u> it on the side of the road. It is not okay to litter."

The underlined word means

  A. throw away.
  B. drive carefully.
  C. pick up.

Best Dressed

Mr. Green's dog has <u>multiple</u> coats. The coats are warm. They keep the dog dry. Mr. Green has enough coats for his dog to wear a different coat every day of the week.

The underlined word means

  A. many.
  B. ugly.
  C. secret.

Name _____ **Date** _____

Garden Fresh

Both Lance and Gale had gardens. The gardens were in their back yards. Lance and Gale grew different kinds of vegetables. Lance had a lot of lettuce. Gale had more tomatoes than she could eat. The two children agreed to a vegetable <u>exchange</u>. This way, they could each enjoy both kinds.

Which word can best replace the underlined word?

  A. race
  B. fight
  C. trade

Little Ones

Animal <u>offspring</u> often look like their parents. For example, bear cubs look like the adult bears. Kittens look like the adult cats. Puppies look like the adult dogs.

Which word can best replace the underlined word?

  A. food
  B. babies
  C. homes

Name _____   **Date** _____

Last Man Standing

I played a game of tug-of-war. I had to <u>release</u> the rope after one minute. It was too hard to hang on to it any longer.

The underlined word means

A. hold.

B. let go.

C. tie.

Young Authors

I like to write. I have fun when I write about things that didn't happen. My friends have fun writing <u>fiction</u> stories, too.

The underlined word means

A. sad.

B. true.

C. made-up.

Name _____ Date _____

What's for Dinner?

Lily could not believe her eyes. People were eating fried spiders! Lily said, "I will try one." Lily only took a tiny <u>nibble</u>. Then she said, "I like it!" and ate the rest with one huge bite.

The underlined word means

A. a small bite or tiny bit.

B. a big gulp or huge swallow.

C. a bug or tasty dish.

Holiday Feast

The Sing family had a big Thanksgiving dinner. They had a big turkey. They had lots of potatoes. They had lots of pie. There was an <u>excess</u> amount of food. There was a lot left over. The Sing family ate leftovers for days.

The underlined word means

A. almost none.

B. too much.

C. not enough.

Name _____ Date _____

Give Dad a Hand

Dad wanted my help. He asked me if I could <u>transfer</u> the books from the table to the bookshelf. Dad wanted the books back where they belong.

The underlined word means

A. write.

B. read.

C. move.

Old News

Ty has a favorite magazine. The magazine comes out once a month. Ty does not have the <u>current</u> issue. The magazine Ty has is a few months old.

Which word can best replace the underlined word?

A. newest

B. past

C. wrinkled

Name _____   Date _____

Lunch Break

Paige and Joe were playing a game. They wanted to keep playing, but they had to stop to eat lunch. Paige and Joe ate quickly. They ate fast because they wanted to <u>continue</u> playing.

Which word(s) can best replace the underlined word?

A. keep on

B. stop

C. put off

Out with the Old

Piper and Aiden went on a walk. They saw an old building. "They are going to <u>demolish</u> that building," Piper said. "It is too old and unsafe." One week later, the building was torn down.

Which word can best replace the underlined word?

A. build

B. invent

C. destroy

Name _____ Date _____

Circle **fact** or **opinion**.

Check a Calendar

A week has seven days.
Is this statement a **fact** or an **opinion**?

Funday Monday

Monday is the best day of the week.
Is this statement a **fact** or an **opinion**?

May I Borrow Those?

People look smart when they wear glasses.
Is this statement a **fact** or an **opinion**?

Fine Print

People wear glasses to help them see well.
Is this statement a **fact** or an **opinion**?

Dinner Time

The best time to eat dinner is at 6:00 p.m.
Is this statement a **fact** or an **opinion**?

Make New Friends

Playing sports is the best way to make new friends.
Is this statement a **fact** or an **opinion**?

Big Dog, Little Dog

Dogs come in all different sizes and colors.
Is this statement a **fact** or an **opinion**?

The Cat's Meow

Cats are the prettiest animals.
Is this statement a **fact** or an **opinion**?

Name _____ Date _____

Circle **fact** or **opinion**.

Scary Seas

Sharks are the scariest-looking fish in the sea.
    Is this statement a **fact** or an **opinion**?

Mental Math

Five plus five is ten.
    Is this statement a **fact** or an **opinion**?

Ask Picasso

Mixing yellow paint with blue paint makes green paint.
    Is this statement a **fact** or an **opinion**?

Storytellers

A good story should have a happy ending.
    Is this statement a **fact** or an **opinion**?

That's a Big Omelet!

A dozen eggs is the same as 12 eggs.
    Is this statement a **fact** or an **opinion**?

Junior Pilot

Making paper airplanes is more fun than coloring.
    Is this statement a **fact** or an **opinion**?

Pleasant Plants

All plants need water and sunlight.
    Is this statement a **fact** or an **opinion**?

Road Trip!

Changing a flat tire is very difficult.
    Is this statement a **fact** or an **opinion**?

Name _____ Date _____

Zoo Babies
Which statement is a **fact**?
- A. Baby lions are prettier than baby panda bears.
- B. Baby lions and baby panda bears are called cubs.

No-Fly Zone
Which statement is an **opinion**?
- A. Some birds, like the ostrich and the penguin, can't fly.
- B. Birds that cannot fly would make great pets.

Corny Comparison
Which statement is a **fact**?
- A. Corn kernels grow on a part of the plant called the ear.
- B. Popped corn is better than corn on the cob.

Math Facts
Which statement is an **opinion**?
- A. Learning how to add is easier than learning how to subtract.
- B. In math, you learn how to add and subtract.

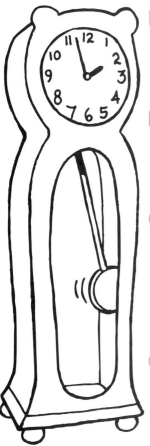

It's Tricky
Which statement is a **fact**?
- A. Many animals, such as dogs, can be trained to do tricks.
- B. Teaching a dog to "shake hands" with you is easy.

No Bib, No Service
Which statement is an **opinion**?
- A. All babies should wear a bib all day long.
- B. A bib helps keep a baby's shirt from getting food or dirt on it.

Colors of the World
Which statement is a **fact**?
- A. The United States has the three best colors—red, white, and blue—on its flag.
- B. Switzerland is the only country in the world with a square flag.

Clock Talk
Which statement is an **opinion**?
- A. On a clock, the minute hand is longer than the hour hand.
- B. Telling time on a clock with hands is very difficult.

Name _____ **Date** _____

Eye Caramba!

Which statement is a **fact**?

    A. Having big eyes is much better than having big ears.

    B. The animal with the largest eyes is the squid. Some squids have eyes the size of dinner plates!

Tomato Time

Which statement is an **opinion**?

    A. Tomatoes should only be used for pizza sauce and ketchup.

    B. Tomatoes were first grown in the Americas.

Healthy Habits

Which statement is a **fact**?

    A. Some people run to stay in shape.

    B. Running is the best way to stay in shape.

Paper Views

Which statement is an **opinion**?

    A. Papermaking was first invented in China.

    B. Students should not use so much paper at school.

It's Black and White

Which statement is a **fact**?

    A. Zebras are the best-looking horses.

    B. Zebras are members of the horse family.

Hip to Be Square

Which statement is an **opinion**?

    A. A square is the hardest shape to draw correctly.

    B. The four sides of a square all have the same length.

A Dog's Worst Friend

Which statement is a **fact**?

    A. A dog can get fleas if it rolls around in the grass.

    B. Dogs are the best choice for a pet.

A Pickle of a Problem

Which statement is an **opinion**?

    A. Sweet pickles are the best choice for a turkey sandwich.

    B. Pickles are made from cucumbers.

Name _____   Date _____

Ouch!

Erin touched the hot pan and
<u>burned her finger</u>.

> The underlined phrase is the
>
> **A.** cause.   **B.** effect.

Fourth of July

<u>The children screamed</u> when they heard the loud boom from
the fireworks.

> The underlined phrase is the
>
> **A.** cause.   **B.** effect.

BBQ Smile

<u>I had corn stuck in my teeth</u>, so I flossed my teeth to get it out.

> The underlined phrase is the
>
> **A.** cause.   **B.** effect.

Pucker Up!

<u>The girl licked the lemon</u> and made a funny face.

> The underlined phrase is the
>
> **A.** cause.   **B.** effect.

Scooter Scotty

<u>Scotty scraped his knee</u> when he fell off his scooter.

> The underlined phrase is the
>
> **A.** cause.   **B.** effect.

Name _____ **Date** _____

First Things First

<u>Olivia can't go to the park</u> because she is not done with her chores.

> The underlined phrase is the
>
> **A.** cause. **B.** effect.

Money Toss

Carlos threw the dime into the pool, and <u>it sank to the bottom</u>.

> The underlined phrase is the
>
> **A.** cause. **B.** effect.

Soup Night

<u>Hannah knew soup was for dinner</u>, so she took out some spoons.

> The underlined phrase is the
>
> **A.** cause. **B.** effect.

Just What I Wanted!

<u>Ryan jumped up and down with joy</u> when he opened his present.

> The underlined phrase is the
>
> **A.** cause. **B.** effect.

Safe Drivers

<u>The traffic light turned yellow</u>, so all the cars slowed to a stop.

> The underlined phrase is the
>
> **A.** cause. **B.** effect.

Name _____ Date _____

A Day at the Park

<u>We were able to fly our kite</u> since it was a windy day.

The underlined phrase is the

A. cause.　　　　　　**B.** effect.

Storm Watch

The streets filled up with water when <u>the big storm came</u>.

The underlined phrase is the

A. cause.　　　　　　　　　**B.** effect.

Make a Wish

<u>Johnny lit the candles on Harper's birthday cake</u>, and then Harper blew them all out.

The underlined phrase is the

A. cause.　　　　　　　　　**B.** effect.

Always Look Both Ways

The bus honked its horn when <u>the man rode his bicycle into the street</u>.

The underlined phrase is the

A. cause.　　　　　　　　　**B.** effect.

Buried Bones

When the dog owner gave her dog a bone, <u>the dog ran into the back yard and buried it next to the fence</u>.

The underlined phrase is the

A. cause.　　　　　　　　　**B.** effect.

All Tripped Up

Ian was running fast. He noticed his shoelaces had untied. Ian didn't stop to tie his shoelaces. He kept running. <u>Ian stepped on his shoelace while running</u> and fell down.

The underlined statement is the **CAUSE**.
What is the **EFFECT**?

   A. Ian tied his shoelaces.
   B. Ian kept running.
   C. Ian fell down.

Morning Appetite

Zoe was very hungry when she woke up. She went straight to the kitchen to get something to eat. <u>She ate two bowls of cereal and two pieces of toast</u>! Zoe felt much better after she ate.

The underlined statement is the **EFFECT**.
What is the **CAUSE**?

   A. Zoe's mom told her to.
   B. Zoe was very hungry.
   C. Zoe went to the kitchen.

Name _____ Date _____

Unprepared

Carter went for a walk with his dad. While they were on their way back home, <u>it started raining really hard</u>. Carter and his dad didn't have an umbrella with them. They got soaked! Carter and his dad ran home and changed into dry clothes.

The underlined statement is the **CAUSE**.
What is the **EFFECT**?

   A. Carter and his dad got really wet.
   B. Carter and his dad went for a walk.
   C. Carter and his dad got out their umbrella.

Feeling Shy

Our pet dog Sparky did not want to be seen today. This morning I saw him under a chair. Sparky hid under a blanket, too. I lifted up the blanket. <u>Sparky quickly ran outside</u>.

The underlined statement is the **EFFECT**.
What is the **CAUSE**?

   A. Sparky saw a cat.
   B. I saw him under a chair.
   C. I lifted up the blanket.

Name _____ **Date** _____

Looking Up

<u>Hailey looked into the telescope</u>. She saw a planet. It was Jupiter. Then Hailey saw something else. She saw five of Jupiter's moons! Hailey thought, "It must be strange to have more than one moon."

The underlined statement is the **CAUSE**.
What is the **EFFECT**?

   A. Hailey saw five of Jupiter's moons.
   B. Hailey wanted to see more moons.
   C. Hailey looked at more planets.

A Friendly Contest

<u>Tran's legs were very tired</u>. Earlier that day, Tran and his friends had a contest. They wanted to see who could run the most laps around the track without stopping. Tran ran ten laps and won the contest!

The underlined statement is the **EFFECT**.
What is the **CAUSE**?

   A. Tran ran to school and back home.
   B. Tran won a jumping contest.
   C. Tran did a lot of running.

Name _____   Date _____

Oh, Brother!

Gavin built a castle out of building blocks. He worked hard to build the castle. <u>Gavin's older brother knocked down the castle.</u> Gavin got very upset.

The underlined statement is the **CAUSE**. What is the **EFFECT**?

- **A.** Gavin worked hard.
- **B.** Gavin got very upset.
- **C.** Gavin built a castle.

Keeping It Cool

Alana turned on the hose in her back yard. It was very hot outside, and Alana wanted to cool down. Alana splashed in the water for a long time. <u>She got soaking wet.</u> After a while, Alana said, "Now I need to warm up!"

The underlined statement is the **EFFECT**. What is the **CAUSE**?

- **A.** Alana turned on the water.
- **B.** Alana splashed in the water.
- **C.** Alana needed to warm up.

Name _____   **Date** _____

Take Me Out to the Ballgame

Douglas was the first player up to bat for his baseball team. The pitcher threw the first pitch. Douglas swung and hit the ball deep into left field. <u>One of the outfielders caught the ball.</u> "Out!" shouted the umpire.

> The underlined statement is the **CAUSE**.
> What is the **EFFECT**?
>
>   **A.** Douglas was out.
>   **B.** Douglas swung the bat.
>   **C.** Douglas was up to bat.

Cammy the Camel

My name is Cammy. I am a camel that walks up and down sand dunes. The wind blows, stirring up the sand, but <u>my eyes are safe from the sand</u>. You have one row of eyelashes, but I have two! My extra row of eyelashes helps keep sand out of my eyes. My lashes are extra-long, too!

> The underlined statement is the **EFFECT**.
> What is the **CAUSE**?
>
>   **A.** Cammy walks up and down sand dunes.
>   **B.** Cammy has an extra row of long eyelashes.
>   **C.** The wind blows, stirring up the sand.

Name _____   **Date** _____

Too Much Salt!

Even though her dad told her not to, <u>Molly added extra salt to her dinner</u>. Molly took a bite of her pasta and then spit it out. It was way too salty. Molly didn't like how it tasted anymore.

The underlined statement is the **CAUSE**.
What is the **EFFECT**?

 A. Molly liked how her pasta tasted with salt.
 B. Molly got in trouble with her dad.
 C. Molly's food tasted too salty.

Falling Leaves

Summer was over. Now it was fall. The leaves on the trees changed color. Then they dropped to the ground. The twins, Mia and Damian, worked hard raking up the leaves into a big pile. When they were done, their father came out and lit the leaves on fire. <u>Now the twins could toast marshmallows on their leaf bonfire</u>!

The underlined statement is the **EFFECT**.
What is the **CAUSE**?

 A. The leaves on the trees changed color.
 B. Summer was over.
 C. The twins' father lit the leaves on fire.

Name _____ **Date** _____

Worst Flight Ever

The plane shook! Eli thought the wings would fall off. <u>The plane reached inside the eye of the hurricane</u>, and it stopped shaking. Everything was calm inside the eye of the hurricane. Eli did not relax for long. Now he had to fly the plane out of the eye and back into the storm.

The underlined statement is the **CAUSE**.
What is the **EFFECT**?

  A. The plane stopped shaking.
  B. The plane started to shake.
  C. The wings fell off.

Little Bee, Big Buzz

A buzzing sound came from near the window. <u>Benjamin went to see what it was</u>. He stared out the window, but he didn't see what was making the sound. Then Benjamin saw something small moving by the window. It was a bee trying to get out.

The underlined statement is the **EFFECT**.
What is the **CAUSE**?

  A. Benjamin saw something small.
  B. Benjamin didn't see anything.
  C. Benjamin heard a buzzing sound.

Name _____ **Date** _____

Extra Recess

Recess is fifteen minutes long most days. My friends and I play tag. Today, the bell was late. <u>The bell didn't ring to end recess until twenty minutes had gone by</u>. We got to play for an extra five minutes.

The underlined statement is the **CAUSE**.
What is the **EFFECT**?

  A. We lined up at the door.
  B. We got to play longer.
  C. We played tag.

Now Where Was I?

Layla reads a few pages every night from her chapter book. Last night, she forgot to put her bookmark in when she was done. <u>Now she doesn't remember what page she is on</u>. She will have to reread some pages to find out where she left off.

The underlined statement is the **EFFECT**.
What is the **CAUSE**?

  A. Layla didn't use a bookmark.
  B. Layla reads a few pages every night.
  C. Layla will have to reread some pages.

Name _____ **Date** _____

Spilled Milk

1. Meg was drinking her milk as she walked down the hall.

2. Meg tripped over her sister's shoes and fell down.

3. The milk spilled all over the living room floor.

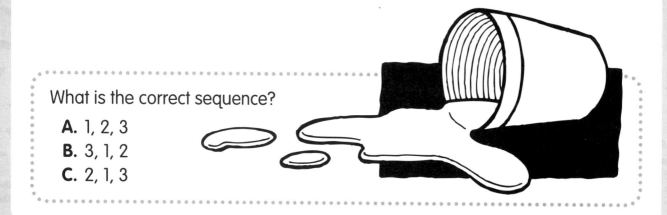

What is the correct sequence?
- **A.** 1, 2, 3
- **B.** 3, 1, 2
- **C.** 2, 1, 3

Muddy Surprise

1. Brayden came home and noticed that his dog had rolled in the mud.

2. Brayden was so happy to have a clean dog to play with.

3. Brayden decided to give his dog a bath to clean off the mud.

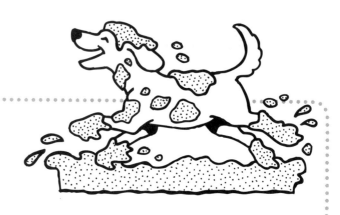

Which sentence comes **second**?
- **A.** Sentence 1
- **B.** Sentence 2
- **C.** Sentence 3

Name _____ **Date** _____

Cleaning My Room

1. The first thing I did was make my bed.

2. Then I put all my toys, books, and clothes where they belong.

3. I woke up early this morning and started cleaning my room.

Which sentence comes **first**?

  A. Sentence 1
  B. Sentence 2
  C. Sentence 3

Not a Great Plan

1. The phone rang, so Mr. Hippo put his ice-cream bar on a paper plate.

2. Mr. Hippo took the ice-cream bar out of the freezer.

3. By the time Mr. Hippo got off the phone, the ice-cream bar had melted.

What is the correct sequence?

  A. 3, 1, 2
  B. 2, 1, 3
  C. 1, 2, 3

Name _____ Date _____

New Faces

1. The eggs hatched, and out came five baby chicks.

2. The mother bird sat on her eggs for several days.

3. The mother bird laid her eggs in the nest that was up high in the tree.

What is the correct sequence?

  A. 1, 2, 3
  B. 3, 2, 1
  C. 3, 1, 2

Milky Mess

1. Ms. Zebra quickly reached for a napkin to wipe up the milk.

2. Ms. Zebra spilled her milk on the table during lunch.

3. Ms. Zebra cleaned it all up before the milk could go over the edge.

What is the correct sequence?

  A. 2, 1, 3
  B. 1, 3, 2
  C. 2, 3, 1

Name _____ **Date** _____

Juice Party

1. We each drank a can of juice with our dinner.

2. Afterwards, we threw the cans into the recycling bin.

3. Mom bought six small cans of apple juice.

Which sentence comes **second**?

- **A.** Sentence 1
- **B.** Sentence 2
- **C.** Sentence 3

Baby on the Move

1. Three months later, when Claire was eight months old, she started crawling.

2. Just after her first birthday, Claire could walk from one room to the next.

3. Baby Claire learned to sit up on her own when she was five months old.

Which sentence comes **first**?

- **A.** Sentence 1
- **B.** Sentence 2
- **C.** Sentence 3

Name _____ **Date** _____

Learning the Rules

1. Dale and his dad enjoyed playing the new game.

2. Dale got a game for his birthday that he'd never played before.

3. Dale read the game directions with his dad.

Which sentence comes **last**?

  A. Sentence 1
  B. Sentence 2
  C. Sentence 3

Safety First

1. Ryder rode over a rock and fell on the sidewalk.

2. Ryder's head did not get hurt because he was wearing his helmet.

3. Ryder put on his helmet to go for a bike ride.

Which sentence comes **last**?

  A. Sentence 1
  B. Sentence 2
  C. Sentence 3

Name _____ **Date** _____

Race in the Park

1. The neighborhood kids stood behind the starting line at the park.

2. The children began running as fast as they could.

3. Violet yelled to the children, "On your mark. Get set. Go!"

What is the correct sequence?

  A. 3, 1, 2
  B. 1, 3, 2
  C. 1, 2, 3

Fear Factor

1. Holding up the snake, the zookeeper asked if anyone else would like to hold it.

2. Luis didn't like when the zookeeper took the big snake out of its cage.

3. Luis was surprised that the snake felt dry, not slimy.

What is the correct sequence?

  A. 1, 2, 3
  B. 2, 3, 1
  C. 2, 1, 3

Name _____ **Date** _____

Pool Party

1. The children played games after they were done eating.

2. The pool party started at noon.

3. Lunch was served about an hour after people got there.

Which sentence comes **first**?

   A. Sentence 1
   B. Sentence 2
   C. Sentence 3

Swimming Lessons

1. Kimberly climbed up the ladder to the diving board.

2. Kimberly dove headfirst into the 12-foot-deep pool.

3. When Kimberly swam up, she said, "I can't wait to dive in again!"

Which sentence comes **first**?

   A. Sentence 1
   B. Sentence 2
   C. Sentence 3

Name _____ Date _____

Saved by the Socks

1. Wyatt fell down once when he was learning how to skate, but he didn't hurt his knees.

2. Wyatt said, "Most likely, I will fall down a few times when I learn how to skate, so I need a plan."

3. Wyatt tied some soft socks around his knees.

What is the correct sequence?
- **A.** 1, 3, 2
- **B.** 1, 2, 3
- **C.** 2, 3, 1

Smells Like Breakfast

1. Dad woke up early and began to make breakfast.

2. I could smell bacon cooking as soon as I woke up.

3. I put eggs and bacon on bread and had a breakfast sandwich.

What is the correct sequence?
- **A.** 2, 3, 1
- **B.** 1, 2, 3
- **C.** 3, 1, 2

Name _____ **Date** _____

Mark's New Look

1. On the first day of second grade, Mark's friends were shocked at how short his hair was.

2. Mark's parents took him to get a haircut a week before he started school.

3. Mark had let his hair grow so long that it touched his shoulders.

Which sentence comes **last**?

A. Sentence 1
B. Sentence 2
C. Sentence 3

A Sight for Sore Eyes

1. Soon after the ship was loaded, the sailors set sail for a new land.

2. The sailors got the ship ready for a long voyage.

3. The sailors cheered at the sight of the new land.

Which sentence comes **last**?

A. Sentence 1
B. Sentence 2
C. Sentence 3

Name _____   **Date** _____

Dad to the Rescue

1. Joan forgot her homework at home.

2. Joan asked her dad if he could bring her homework to school for her.

3. Joan used the phone in the school office to call her dad.

What is the correct sequence?

   A. 3, 2, 1
   B. 2, 3, 1
   C. 1, 3, 2

Farm Friends

1. The farmer sheared the sheep, cutting off all their wool.

2. The freshly shorn wool was sold and made into socks.

3. The farmer's dog chased the sheep into the barn.

What is the correct sequence?

   A. 3, 1, 2
   B. 3, 2, 1
   C. 2, 1, 3

Name _____ Date _____

Our Own Pumpkin Patch

1. The seeds sprouted into small, green plants.

2. Ten pumpkin seeds were planted in a row in the garden.

3. Within a few weeks, the pumpkin vines were all over the garden.

What is the correct sequence?

A. 2, 1, 3
B. 3, 2, 1
C. 2, 3, 1

Evan's Clean Teeth

1. The first thing Evan does when he brushes his teeth is wet his toothbrush.

2. He brushes his teeth for two minutes before rinsing.

3. He squeezes on a small amount of toothpaste.

What is the correct sequence?

A. 2, 1, 3
B. 3, 2, 1
C. 1, 3, 2

Is It Magic?

1. A small magnet was put on top of a paper plate.

2. A paper clip was held up to the paper plate on the other side.

3. The paper clip stayed on the bottom of the plate even when no one was holding it.

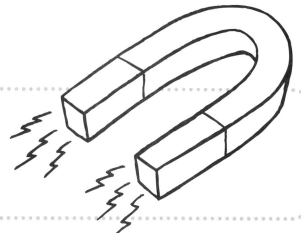

What is the correct sequence?

  A. 1, 3, 2
  B. 1, 2, 3
  C. 2, 1, 3

Too Cold!

1. By the time John remembered to get his drink, he had a cup of ice.

2. To get the water colder, John placed the cup in the freezer.

3. John poured himself a cup of water. The water was not as cold as John liked.

What is the correct sequence?

  A. 2, 3, 1
  B. 3, 2, 1
  C. 1, 2, 3

Name _____ Date _____

A Net Full of Water

1. Everyone laughed at Allison when she said, "I can hold water in a net. Just watch me."

2. Allison took out ice cubes and put them in a net.

3. Allison went to the freezer.

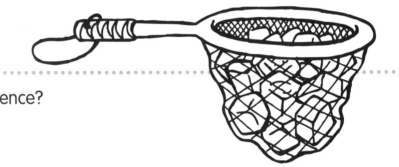

What is the correct sequence?

   A. 3, 2, 1

   B. 1, 2, 3

   C. 1, 3, 2

Playful Puppy

1. The puppy yelped a lot during lunch and pawed at everyone's feet.

2. The family sat down to have a nice, quiet lunch.

3. Everyone thought the lunch would have been quieter if the puppy had been put outside.

What is the correct sequence?

   A. 2, 1, 3

   B. 1, 2, 3

   C. 3, 2, 1

Name _____ **Date** _____

Mail from a Friend

1. Patty made a birthday card for her friend Ashley.

2. Ashley was happy to get a birthday card in the mail.

3. Patty put the card in an envelope and mailed it to her friend.

What is the correct sequence?

A. 1, 3, 2

B. 1, 2, 3

C. 3, 2, 1

Building Castles

1. Ana took two pails and her shovel with her to the beach.

2. Ana flipped over the pails and started to build a large sandcastle.

3. At the beach, Ana used her shovel to dig in the wet sand and fill the pails.

What is the correct sequence?

A. 1, 2, 3

B. 1, 3, 2

C. 3, 2, 1

Name _____ **Date** _____

Junior Banker

1. That night, Luke put the four cents that he had gotten back in change into his piggy bank.

2. On Tuesday, Luke took out nine dimes from his piggy bank to buy gum.

3. Luke put three dollars in coins into his piggy bank on Monday.

Which sentence comes **first**?

   A. Sentence 1
   B. Sentence 2
   C. Sentence 3

Tales of Adventure

1. Young Hee thought that one day he would write a book about knights, too.

2. In the book, Greg saw knights on horses.

3. Young Hee read a book about a boy named Greg who could travel back in time.

Which sentence comes **second**?

   A. Sentence 1
   B. Sentence 2
   C. Sentence 3

Name _____ Date _____

Terry's Busy Day

Terry woke up from his nap and made his bed. He was still tired from playing soccer all morning. Terry made a snack to eat, and then he watched a TV show. Terry did some homework before dinner. Soon it was time for bed.

Most likely, **when** did Terry make his bed?

   A. in the afternoon
   B. in the morning
   C. at night

First Day of Practice

Aubrey took her ball with her to practice. Thirteen other girls were there, too. Each girl was holding a ball. A woman told the girls to run up the court and back while dribbling the balls. Then the woman told them to practice shooting free throws. Aubrey made a basket on her first try.

Most likely, **who** is the woman?

   A. Aubrey's teacher
   B. Aubrey's grandma
   C. Aubrey's coach

Name _____   **Date** _____

Cold Tub

"Let's go into the hot tub," said Brad. Brad's dad turned on the heater to warm up the water. He told Brad it would take at least 20 minutes to get warm. Brad didn't want to wait. He quickly put on his bathing suit and got into the water. After only two seconds, he jumped out of the water. "That's not a hot tub at all!" said Brad, shivering.

Most likely, **why** did Brad jump out of the water?

 A. The water was too hot.
 B. The water was too cold.
 C. Brad's dad told him to get out.

A Stinky Cat?

Parker and Kayla were walking along a road. They spotted a black cat with a thick, white stripe on its back. Kayla walked closer to it and tried to pet it. "Oh, no," screamed Kayla. "That cat is not a cat at all! It's a skunk!" Parker and Kayla ran away as quickly as they could.

Most likely, **why** did Parker and Kayla run away so quickly?

 A. They didn't want to be late for dinner.
 B. They didn't want to get sprayed by the skunk.
 C. They wanted the skunk to chase them.

Name _____   **Date** _____

Band Practice

Miguel strummed his guitar. Blake was sitting near Miguel. Blake played the piano. Together, they played a nice tune. Maria was standing in the front. She was holding a microphone. She took a deep breath.

Most likely, **what** will Maria do?

   A. play an instrument
   B. dance to the music
   C. sing a song

Beat the Heat

In the summer, it is much too hot for Mike to be outside while the sun is out. So, Mike runs while it is still dark out. Mike turns around and runs back home when he sees the sun start to come up. Mike runs every day. He is training to run a 13-mile race.

Most likely, **when** does Mike run?

   A. early in the morning
   B. in the middle of the day
   C. late at night

Name _____ **Date** _____

No Ordinary Job

Brinn unzipped her sleeping bag. She unstrapped the belt around her. Then Brinn wiggled out of her sleeping bag. She began to float. Brinn needed to get her toothbrush wet, but there was no running water. Instead, Brinn wet her toothbrush by pushing water up a straw from a bag. Next, Brinn put toothpaste on her brush. After brushing, Brinn did not spit. She swallowed what was in her mouth.

Most likely, **where** is Brinn?

- **A.** in an airplane
- **B.** at her grandmother's house
- **C.** in space

A Great Day in Mudville

The score was tied—seven to seven. The pitcher threw a fastball. Julian swung the bat as hard as he could. He hit the ball hard, and it went sailing through the air. Julian's parents cheered as they watched from their seats. The ball went over the fence. Julian dropped his bat and ran, scoring a point for his team. Then he walked over and gave his parents high-fives.

Most likely, **where** were Julian's parents?

- **A.** at a place that shows sports on TV
- **B.** at a baseball game
- **C.** at a basketball game

Name _____ **Date** _____

Practice Makes Perfect

Grant went to school and jumped out of a window. Grant also ran with a heavy tool. The tool weighed 50 pounds, but Grant could not drop it. Then Grant practiced dragging a big, heavy dummy. Grant ran up and down stairs, too. Grant dragged a big hose when he ran up and down the stairs. Finally, Grant had to practice pushing big, heavy doors open.

Most likely, **what** does Grant go to school for?

   A. to learn how to be a firefighter
   B. to learn how to be a janitor
   C. to learn how to be a cook

Celebration Day

Carmen and Tom put on their bathing suits and went to a party at the beach. All the children got buckets and shovels when they arrived. Carmen and Tom started building sandcastles. Then Carmen and her friends played in the waves. Tom looked for shells. Afterwards, they all sat on the sand and ate red, white, and blue cake.

Most likely, **what** holiday were Carmen and Tom celebrating?

   A. Christmas
   B. the Fourth of July
   C. Valentine's Day

Name _____ Date _____

Lincoln's Books

Lincoln walked in through the front door. Books were everywhere he looked. He flipped through one book about animals. Lincoln really liked all the pictures. He decided to read it at home. Lincoln took the book to the counter and gave the lady his card. She said he had to bring the book back in three weeks. If Lincoln forgot, he would have to pay a fine for being late.

Most likely, **where** was Lincoln?

A. at a bookstore
B. at a zoo
C. at a library

Late-Night Party

Joy went to a party. She got there at nine o'clock in the evening. Everyone was playing games, eating snacks, and drinking hot chocolate. Joy stayed at the party for a long time. When it was midnight, everyone cheered. When she got home, it was the next day. She was so tired that she went straight to bed.

Most likely, **what** kind of party did Joy go to?

A. a New Year's Eve party
B. a birthday party
C. a Christmas party

Name _____ **Date** _____

Slow Down!

Whoosh! The car sped by the school. Whoosh! The car raced past the hospital. Whoosh! The car sped through a red light. Whoosh! Another car raced through a crosswalk. Mr. Khan said, "These cars are not going the speed limit. Cars should not be racing past the school and past the hospital. Cars should not be racing through red lights or crosswalks. I need to call someone who can give tickets to the drivers. I need to call someone who can make this stop."

Most likely, **whom** will Mr. Khan call?
- **A.** a police officer
- **B.** a mail carrier
- **C.** a firefighter

Lights Out

Mr. and Mrs. Lopez arrived just in time. Most of the seats in the room were taken. They found two empty seats next to each other and sat down. Soon, all the lights went out, and something started playing on the big screen. Mr. and Mrs. Lopez sat back and watched.

Most likely, **where** were Mr. and Mrs. Lopez?
- **A.** at home
- **B.** at a movie theater
- **C.** at a play

Name _____ Date _____

Some Assembly Required

Hope's new toy came in the mail. She opened up the box and took out all the pieces. Hope didn't know how to put it together. She read some papers that were inside the box. Hope did exactly what the papers said. The last thing the papers said to do was put in batteries. When Hope turned the switch on, her new toy was working perfectly. Hope's brother asked if he could play with it, too.

Most likely, **how** did Hope put the toy together?

A. Hope's brother helped her put it together.
B. Hope read a story about a kid with a toy like hers.
C. Hope followed the instructions carefully.

No, Thanks

One day, Dina ate a candy bar with nuts in it. She loved the taste, but it gave her a bad rash. She didn't know why. A month later, Dina ate a different candy bar with nuts in it, and she got an even worse rash. The next week, Dina went to her friend's house. When her friend offered her an ice-cream cone with nuts on top, Dina said, "No, thanks."

Most likely, **why** did Dina not want the ice cream?

A. She was afraid the nuts would give her a rash.
B. She did not like the taste of nuts.
C. She wanted to eat a candy bar with nuts instead.

Name _____ Date _____

Snow Day

All of the second grade classes in Sunnyside School went on a field trip. Everyone rode on the bus up a winding road. When they got there, they all put on jackets, hats, and gloves. The students had fun spending the day in the snow. At the end of the day, the students were cold and tired.

Most likely, **what** did the students do on their field trip?

  A. swimming
  B. biking
  C. sledding

It's Not a Dog

"I am thinking of an animal," Dylan said. "The female is called a hen. This animal has an ink sac. When this animal feels scared, it spews out a squirt of dark liquid. The liquid looks like dark ink. This animal likes to hide behind rocks or in caves. It also has suckers on its eight arms."

Most likely, **what** animal is Dylan talking about?

  A. a chicken
  B. an octopus
  C. a spider

Stinky Cheese

Ella walked into the kitchen and plugged her nose. "What is that awful smell?" she asked. Ella's mom was cooking a new recipe. The recipe called for blue cheese. Ella's mom said that the cheese is a little smelly, but it tastes great. When Ella's mom was done cooking, she put some on a plate for Ella to try. Ella took a small bite of the cheese and smiled.

Most likely, **what** did Ella think about the taste of the cheese?

   A. She thought it tasted horrible.
   B. She thought it was too salty.
   C. She thought it tasted great.

A Stormy Night

The storm was still going after two hours. Rain was falling harder and harder. Andrew sat by the window and looked outside. He watched as a flash of light came down from the clouds. A few seconds later, Andrew heard the sound of thunder. Andrew was happy to be dry and warm inside his house.

Most likely, **what** was the flash of light that Andrew saw?

   A. lightning
   B. a car's headlights
   C. someone's flashlight

Name _____ **Date** _____

Too Many Questions

Nicole was sitting at her desk in her room. Her sister was playing a video game in the living room. Nicole wanted to play video games with her. Nicole asked her dad if she could play with her sister. "No," said her dad. "You know you have to turn in the story questions tomorrow. Finish reading the story and answer the questions right now."

Most likely, **what** was Nicole doing?

A. doing homework
B. playing video games
C. cleaning her room

Hearts

Ms. Lam was standing at the front of the room. Everyone was looking at her. She drew two hearts on the board right next to each other. Next, she drew another set of two hearts. Then she drew a third set of two hearts. Ms. Lam looked at the class and asked them to find the total number of hearts. She explained how to find the total in two ways: when adding, $2 + 2 + 2 = 6$ hearts, and when multiplying, 2 hearts $\times$ 3 sets = 6 hearts.

Most likely, **who** is Ms. Lam?

A. an art teacher
B. a science teacher
C. a math teacher

A Well-Earned Reward

Noah really wanted a skateboard. His parents told him they would buy him a skateboard if he earned it. To earn it, Noah had to do a good deed every day for two months. Noah worked hard. He helped neighbors. He helped his parents. He helped his teachers at school. Two months later, Noah's parents took him shopping for a skateboard. Noah was very happy!

Most likely, **what** will Noah do when he gets home?

A. do his homework
B. ride his skateboard
C. play a board game

Two Cold Poles

"There are two poles," Lina said. "There is the North Pole and the South Pole. Both poles are covered in ice, but only the South Pole is on land. The South Pole is on a continent. The North Pole is on a frozen ocean. Polar bears do not live on the same pole as penguins. When explorers go to the pole on the frozen ocean, they have to watch out for polar bears."

Most likely, **where** do explorers see penguins?

A. at the zoo
B. at the South Pole
C. at the North Pole

Name _____   Date _____

The Purple Top

When the bell rang, the students in Mrs. Sun's class lined up to go into the classroom. Paul was wearing blue pants and a white shirt. Eddie was wearing the same thing. Abigail was wearing blue shorts and a white shirt. So was Elizabeth. Brianna was wearing brown pants with a purple shirt. Mrs. Sun called Brianna's mom to bring her a change of clothes.

Most likely, **why** did Brianna need to change her clothes?

   A. Brianna asked Mrs. Sun to call her mom.
   B. Brianna got her clothes dirty on the playground.
   C. Brianna was not wearing the school uniform.

Bus Adventure

An hour after school started, Mr. Moon's class lined up on the sidewalk. Each student was holding a sack lunch. "Quietly, get on the bus and find a seat," said Mr. Moon. "We will leave after everyone is seated and quiet. We should be at the museum in one hour."

Most likely, **why** were the students getting on the bus?

   A. They were going home.
   B. They were going on a field trip.
   C. They were going to school.

Name _____ **Date** _____

Tickets and Smiles

When Seth and Misty arrived, they had big smiles on their faces. They were looking forward to riding the fast rides and playing fun games. The first thing they did was buy a lot of tickets. They used four tickets each to ride the Super Swings. Seth liked it so much that he went on it again. Misty used two tickets to climb a tall rock wall.

Most likely, **where** were Seth and Misty?

   A. at a carnival
   B. at an arcade
   C. at a park

Walking Safely

All the neighborhood kids walk to school together. They have to cross a busy street. Someone is always there when the kids get to this street. This person wears a bright orange vest. This person holds a stop sign. This person walks into the street and stops traffic, so the kids can cross safely.

Most likely, **who** is the person in the orange vest?

   A. the bus driver
   B. the crossing guard
   C. the school principal

Name _____   **Date** _____

The Perfect Food

Josh likes pizza more than any other food in the world. Josh said, "Pizza is the best food because it can have all the different kinds of food you need. It has dairy foods like cheese. You can add meat. Meat is a protein. You can add vegetables. You can add tomatoes or bell peppers. You can even have a pizza that has a fruit topping."

Most likely, **what** type of pizza will Josh likely order?

  A. cheese, pepperoni, olive, and pineapple
  B. pepperoni
  C. cheese

The Girl Who Could See Through Walls

Sasha told her friend Roman that she could see through walls. Roman didn't think Sasha could see through a wall. Then Sasha told Roman that everyone could see through a wall. When you look through a window, you are looking through a wall! Then Sasha told Roman that she had a riddle. She said, "The more I use it, the wetter it gets."

Most likely, **what** is Sasha talking about?

  A. a sock
  B. a pencil
  C. a towel

Bad Habits

Daisy has some bad habits. She doesn't brush her teeth as often as she should. Sometimes, Daisy brushes once a day. Sometimes, she doesn't brush at all. To make things worse, Daisy eats a lot of candy! The dentist told Daisy that she needs to brush more. Daisy has a tooth that is sure to get a cavity if she doesn't change these bad habits of hers. Daisy didn't listen to the dentist.

Predict what will happen.

   A. Daisy will probably get a cavity.
   B. Daisy will probably stop eating candy.
   C. Daisy will probably brush her teeth twice a day.

Something Different

Vincent's mother cooked a new meal for dinner. She found the recipe in one of her cookbooks. When Vincent saw what was for dinner, he didn't want to taste it. Vincent didn't like tasting new foods. "You have to taste it to know whether you like it or not," said Vincent's mom. Vincent took one bite and smiled. "It's great!" said Vincent.

Predict what will happen.

   A. Vincent will not take another bite.
   B. Vincent will ask to eat something else.
   C. Vincent will eat more of his dinner.

Name _____   **Date** _____

A Trip to Star Town

Mr. and Mrs. Baker are driving to Star Town to visit some friends. They and their friends are going to the county fair together. As they get off the highway, there are two big signs. One sign says Star Town is to the left. The other sign says Moon Town is to the right.

Predict what will happen.

A. The Bakers will turn right.
B. The Bakers will turn left.
C. The Bakers will keep driving straight.

Mom Knows Best

William and Kyle were playing baseball in their back yard. Their mom told them to play something else. She didn't want them to break something with the ball. If they did, they would get in trouble. The boys didn't listen. William pitched the ball to Kyle. Kyle swung the bat hard and hit the ball. The ball flew across the yard and broke the window.

Predict what will happen.

A. The boys' mom will be happy.
B. The boys will get in trouble.
C. The boys will play baseball in the front yard.

Name _____   Date _____

Shirt Shopping

Nora was shopping for a new shirt to wear on St. Patrick's Day. She found a white shirt that had green shamrocks on it. It was perfect! Nora tried on a size small and a size medium. The small shirt was too tight. The medium shirt fit her just right. When she got home, Nora took her new shirt out of the bag and noticed that the tag said "small."

Predict what will happen.

   A. The shirt will be too tight.
   B. The shirt will be too big.
   C. The shirt will be just the right size.

Spring Forward

"Daylight saving time starts tomorrow," Ms. Sing said. "We put our clocks one hour ahead in daylight saving time. This way, the mornings have less light, but the evenings have more light. Don't forget to set your clocks one hour ahead!"

The next day, all the children got to school on time. They were in their seats at 8:00 when the bell rang. Then the children looked at the clock on the wall. They began to laugh. The time on the clock was 7:00.

Predict what will happen.

   A. The children will get to go home for an hour.
   B. Ms. Sing's class will start when the mornings have more light.
   C. The clock on the wall will be set one hour ahead.

Name _____ **Date** _____

Too Hot to Play

It was a hot summer day. Carson and Cole came in from playing outside. "It's too hot to play," said Cole. "Let's go buy some ice cream." So the two boys walked to the market at the end of their street. When they got to the store, Cole realized that he forgot to bring the money.

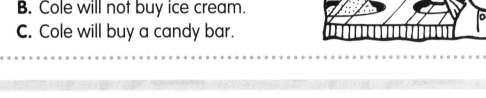

Predict what will happen.

   A. Cole will buy ice cream.
   B. Cole will not buy ice cream.
   C. Cole will buy a candy bar.

Will It Be Windy?

Mrs. Crane is taking Diego and Brooke to a park across town. Diego and Brooke grab two kites and sand toys to take with them. Diego and Brooke want to fly their kites if it's windy at the park. They will play with the sand toys in the sandbox if it's not windy. When they get to the park, it is very windy.

Predict what will happen.

   A. Diego and Brooke will fly their kites.
   B. Diego and Brooke will play in the sandbox.
   C. Diego and Brooke will fight over the sand toys.

Name _____ **Date** _____

Party in the Rain

The local news was on TV. The weatherman said that it would rain on Sunday. Bill looked at his mom and said, "Sunday is Hunter's pool party. If it's raining that day, we won't be able to swim! We'll have to stay inside." While Bill was on his way to Hunter's party, it started raining hard.

Predict what will happen.

- **A.** Bill will play outside at the party.
- **B.** Bill will swim at the party.
- **C.** Bill will play inside at the party.

Wet Paint

Fern was walking to her friend April's house. When Fern got there, she noticed that the fence around the yard looked as though it was a different color. The fence was brown, but Fern remembered the fence being white. Fern was just about to touch the fence when she saw a sign that read, "Wet Paint! Don't Touch!" Fern did not want to get paint on her hands.

Predict what will happen.

- **A.** Fern will touch the fence.
- **B.** Fern will paint the fence.
- **C.** Fern will not touch the fence.

Follow the Recipe

Mr. King was cooking chicken for lunch. The recipe said to heat the oven to 400 degrees. Then, it said to bake the chicken for one hour. Mr. King prepared the chicken just like the recipe said. Then he placed it into the hot oven and set the timer.

Predict what will happen.

    A. The timer will beep in 30 minutes.
    B. The timer will beep in one hour.
    C. The timer will beep when the oven is hot.

A Generous Gift

Tracy had pretty hair. It was long and black. Tracy had been growing it for four years. Tracy wanted to be kind. She wanted to donate her hair. She wanted her hair to go to people who needed wigs. Tracy said she would not cut her hair until it was long enough to give away. If Tracy was going to donate her hair, she had to be able to cut off at least ten inches. Tracy went to the hairdresser. The hairdresser told Tracy that she could easily cut off ten inches.

Predict what will happen.

    A. Tracy will leave the hairdresser with shorter hair.
    B. Tracy will wear a wig.
    C. Tracy will grow her hair ten more inches before she cuts it.

Name _____ **Date** _____

Feeling Crabby

Hermit crabs live in shells. When hermit crabs get too big for their shells, they find a new shell to live in. Austin had a hermit crab. The crab's name was Claw. One day Austin reached into Claw's cage. Austin picked up Claw's shell, but Claw wasn't in it! Austin looked behind some rocks. Then he carefully started to pick up other shells.

Predict what will happen.

- **A.** Austin will find Claw behind some rocks.
- **B.** Austin will find Claw in a bigger shell.
- **C.** Austin will find Claw in a smaller shell.

Simple Signals

Mrs. Snow is an art teacher. When her students are too loud, she gives them a signal to be quiet. She turns the lights off and on a few times. The students know that this means to quiet down. While the students were working on their art projects, the noise level in the class got very loud.

Predict what will happen.

- **A.** Mrs. Snow will shout, "Be quiet!"
- **B.** Mrs. Snow will plug her ears.
- **C.** Mrs. Snow will turn the lights off and on.

Name _____ **Date** _____

Direct Hit!

Eve had a piñata at her birthday party. All the children lined up to get a turn to try to break it. They wondered what it was filled with. Eve told them that it was filled with lollipops and sour candy. Eve got to hit the piñata first. Other children hit the piñata but didn't break it. Then Jason hit the piñata as hard as he could. He broke it on his third swing.

Predict what will happen.
  A. The candy will fall out of the piñata.
  B. Jason will say sorry for breaking the piñata.
  C. The children will eat birthday cake.

Grandma's Gifts

Kellie's grandma does the same thing for Kellie's birthday gift each year. She always gets Kellie a new toy. She also puts dollar bills inside the card. The number of dollar bills Kellie gets is the same number as her age. On her ninth birthday, Kellie got a new toy and nine dollars. Sunday is Kellie's tenth birthday.

Predict what will happen.

  A. Kellie will not get a new toy, but she will get nine dollars.
  B. Kellie will get a new toy and ten dollars.
  C. Kellie will get a new toy and nine dollars.

Name _____ **Date** _____

Green Thumb

Kevin bought a small potted plant. He placed the plant in a sunny spot by his window. Kevin waters his plant every day. Kevin tries hard to take good care of his plant.

Predict what will happen.

   A. The plant will die.
   B. Kevin will lose his plant.
   C. The plant will grow.

Over the Curb

Yori was riding his skateboard on the sidewalk. He was wearing knee and elbow pads. As Yori was riding, he lost his balance. He rode right over the curb. Yori fell down and landed on his knee.

Predict what will happen.

   A. Yori's elbow will be scraped.
   B. Yori's knee will not be scraped.
   C. Yori's knee will be scraped.

Name _____ **Date** _____

Walk to the Top

One year, June went on a trip. She went to New York City. In the city, June went to see the Empire State Building. June wanted to go up to the look-out deck. The look-out deck was 86 stories high. When June got there, she was told the elevator was broken. June decided to walk up the stairs instead. June counted the stairs as she walked. June counted 1,576 stairs in all. The guard at the top told June, "The elevator still does not work."

Predict what will happen.

  A. June will walk down 86 stories.
  B. June will fix the elevator.
  C. June will walk down more than 1,576 stairs.

Without a Bib

Baby Bradley spills food almost every time he eats. His mom puts a bib on him before he eats. Food spills on his bib, not on his shirt. Next week, Baby Bradley will be staying at his Aunt Peggy's house. Aunt Peggy doesn't have a bib to put on him during dinner.

Predict what will happen.

  A. The baby's shirt will probably get dirty.
  B. The baby's shirt will probably stay clean.
  C. The baby will probably not eat his food.

Name _____   **Date** _____

Cookie Milk

Ruby likes eating cookies with milk as a snack. Ruby pours a small glass of milk and puts three small cookies into the milk at the same time. She waits a bit for them to soak up some milk. Then she eats the cookies with a spoon. If she waits too long, the cookies will get soggy and break apart. One day, the phone rang just as Ruby dropped some cookies into a cup of milk. She answered the phone and talked to her friend for ten minutes.

Predict what will happen.

   A. The cookies will not soak up milk.
   B. Ruby will give her friend some cookies.
   C. The cookies will become soggy and break apart.

Bug Boy

Isaac loves to look at bugs. He knows that insects have six legs. He also knows that spiders have eight legs. One day, Isaac and his dad were looking for bugs in the yard. Isaac's dad found an insect that Isaac had never seen before. Isaac used a magnifying glass and counted its legs.

Predict what will happen.

   A. Isaac will count two legs.
   B. Isaac will count six legs.
   C. Isaac will count eight legs.

Name _____ **Date** _____

Good Listener

Kai was helping his mom make cupcakes. Kai's mom mixed the batter. Kai put all the cupcake liners into the cupcake tray. Then Kai's mom started pouring the batter into the liners. Kai asked if he could pour some. His mom told him to only fill up the liners halfway. "If you put too much in, the cupcakes will overflow." Kai poured the batter exactly halfway.

Predict what will happen.

  A. The cupcakes will overflow.
  B. The cupcakes will not overflow.
  C. The cupcakes will burn.

Capital Kids

Two girls named London and Paris were talking. London said, "I was named after a city. My parents met in the city. The city is in England. It is the capital city."

Paris said, "I was named after a city, too. My parents met in the city. The city is in France. It is the capital city."

That night, London's parents told her they were going to take her to France's capital.

Predict what will happen.

  A. London will visit the city where her parents met.
  B. London will visit the capital city of England.
  C. London will visit the city of Paris.

Name _____ Date _____

Big-Girl Bike

Helen has a bike with training wheels on it. Her dad said he'd take the training wheels off when Helen can ride a bike on her own. Helen's friend Lisa doesn't have training wheels on her bike. Helen's dad helped her practice without training wheels using Lisa's bike. Helen learned how to ride Lisa's bike on her own.

Predict what will happen.

A. Helen will trade bikes with Lisa.
B. Helen's dad will buy Helen a new bike.
C. Helen's dad will take the training wheels off of her bike.

Signs

Caleb went to an amusement park with his friend Charlotte. Caleb and Charlotte were excited about all the rides. They walked to the line for the Red Rocket ride. A sign was at the front of the ride. It said that riders had to be at least four feet tall to go on the ride. Both Caleb and Charlotte are taller than four feet.

Predict what will happen.

A. Both Caleb and Charlotte will ride the Red Rocket.
B. Caleb and Charlotte will not ride the Red Rocket.
C. Only Charlotte will ride the Red Rocket.

Name _____ **Date** _____

Time for a Change

The walls in Autumn's bedroom are all white. Autumn doesn't like the way they look anymore. She asked her parents if she could change the color of her room. Autumn's parents took her to the hardware store. There, Autumn picked out two gallons of light-green paint.

Predict what will happen.

 A. Autumn's parents will buy white paint.
 B. Autumn will paint a picture of a bedroom.
 C. Autumn's room will get painted light green.

Night Reader

Bruce loves to read. He is reading a chapter book about a boy who can travel back in time. Bruce reads one chapter from his book every night. Last night, Bruce read chapter seven. He still has five more chapters to read before he finishes the book.

Predict what will happen.

 A. Bruce will read chapter five tonight.
 B. Bruce will read chapter eight tonight.
 C. Bruce will finish the book tonight.

Name _____ **Date** _____

Great Burgers

Julie and her friend Levi were hungry for lunch. Julie said, "Let's go to Great Burgers." Julie had a coupon that read, "Buy one hamburger, get one free." The two friends walked down the street to Great Burgers. Julie bought a hamburger.

Predict what will happen.

   A. Levi will get one hamburger for free.
   B. Levi will order a slice of pizza.
   C. Levi will pay for a hamburger.

Big Baby

Owen read a book about whales. He read that the blue whale is the largest mammal. Adult blue whales can weigh 400,000 pounds. Owen read that a baby blue whale is called a calf. A blue whale calf can weigh 400 pounds at birth. Then, during its first year, the calf can gain 200 pounds a day! Owen's father said that he would take Owen whale watching. When Owen and his dad got on the boat, the captain said they were lucky. A blue whale calf had just been born that morning. He was going to take them to see it!

Predict what will happen.

   A. Owen will see a calf that weighs about 500 pounds.
   B. Owen will see a calf that weighs about 50,000 pounds.
   C. Owen will see a calf that weighs about 500,000 pounds.

Name _____ **Date** _____

The **main idea** is what your story is about. If you are writing a story about birds, you don't want to fill your paper with sentences about elephants!

Think of five things you would like to write about one day. Then say what you *won't* be writing about. Use the same sentence structure as the example.

What My Story Is NOT About

> *Example: I won't be writing about pianos because I will be writing about basketball.*

Remember to use the word *because*!

1. _____ because

    _____

    _____

2. _____

    _____

    _____

3. _____

    _____

    _____

4. _____

    _____

    _____

5. _____

    _____

    _____

Name _____ Date _____

Everyone has different things they like to read and learn about. Think about something that interests you. It could be sports, an animal, a game, or an activity.

I am interested in _____.

What you chose is your **main idea** or topic.

Now write a few sentences or a paragraph in which you include information about your topic. Share what you know and what you think about your topic!

Share Your Interests

_____

_____

_____

_____

_____

_____

_____

_____

_____

_____

_____

_____

_____

Name _____   **Date** _____

A biography is a book about a person. If you read a book called *The Life of George Washington*, what do you think would be the main idea or topic of the book?

All About YOU

_____

You are going to write a short <u>auto</u>biography. An autobiography is written by the person the book is about. This means YOU are the main idea.

Writing about yourself today is too easy, so you will be writing about yourself in 30 years! After saying who you are, say how old you are. Then describe what you do, where you have gone, and an adventure you had.

_____

_____

_____

_____

_____

_____

_____

_____

_____

_____

_____

_____

Name _____   **Date** _____

Imagine you are a sports reporter. You write for a newspaper. This picture is part of your story. Think of a title for the picture. Your title will fit with the **main idea** of your story.

Then write a few sentences using your main idea. Include things that tell more about the main idea.

Extra! Extra! Read All About It!

_____

_____

_____

_____

_____

_____

_____

_____

Name _____ **Date** _____

You are the same, but you are also different!

Look around the classroom and take a good look at your friends. Now, write five sentences about yourself and these friends. In each sentence, describe something that you have in common and something that makes you different.

The Same but Different

> *Example: Alfredo is wearing shoes like mine, but my shoes are red while Alfredo's are green.*

Remember to put a comma before the word *but*. (The first one is done for you.)

1. _____, but

   _____

   _____

2. _____

   _____

   _____

3. _____

   _____

   _____

4. _____

   _____

   _____

5. _____

   _____

   _____

Name _____ **Date** _____

My Unique House

Close your eyes for several seconds and think about your house. Now write down details about your house. You may write anything you want. It can be details about the outside, the inside, the number of rooms, the size, the color, and even what is in it.

Or, if you want, you can describe just one room.

Read your paragraph to your classmates, or share it in a small group. Did you provide enough details so that no one could mix up your house with someone else's?

_____

_____

_____

_____

_____

_____

_____

_____

_____

_____

_____

_____

_____

Name _____   Date _____

One kind of poem is called a **cinquain** (pronounced "*sing-keyn*") poem. You are going to write a cinquain poem about an animal. Think of an animal. Now think of some details about that animal, and then put them into a cinquain poem form.

Sing What?

Bat
Black wings
Flying, soaring, hanging
They eat nasty mosquitoes.
Night

Octopus
Very smart
Crawling, swimming, hiding
They can use tools!
Invertebrate

Line 1: one word title

Line 2: two words that describe the title (often using adjectives)

Line 3: three words that tell the reader more about the subject. Often, these words end in "–ing."

Line 4: four words that show feelings or something good or bad about the title. The words can be individual words or a phrase.

Line 5: another word for the title

Line 1: _____

Line 2: _____   _____

Line 3: _____   _____   _____

Line 4: _____   _____   _____   _____

Line 5: _____

Share your cinquain with a classmate!

Name _____ **Date** _____

Look Closer

Look carefully at the picture for as many details as you can. In the space below, write three details.

1. _____

_____

2. _____

_____

3. _____

_____

Now use your details to write a paragraph about the scene in this picture.

_____

_____

_____

_____

_____

_____

_____

Name _____   Date _____

Sounds Familiar

When reading a story, sometimes the writer does not tell you exactly where someone is or what is happening. You have to figure it out, just like sometimes you have to figure out new words by what you read before and after the new word.

Think of a place. It can be a grocery store, a circus, a farm, your dinner table, your classroom, the playground, a zoo—any place you want!

Now, write down some sentences in which you describe the *sounds* you hear and who is making them. Don't say where you are!

When you are quoting people directly, put their words inside quotation marks.

Example: "Here you go," said the lady who gave me a carton of milk.

1. _____

_____

_____

2. _____

_____

_____

3. _____

_____

_____

4. _____

_____

_____

5. _____

_____

_____

Turn to a classmate and read what you wrote. Could they figure out what place you were writing about? Draw a star next to the sentence you think was your best clue.

Think of an animal. Write down some information about the animal. You might mention how it looks, what it sounds like, where it lives, what it eats, and what it does. Don't say what the animal is!

Read your sentences to your classmates. How many sentences did they have to hear before they knew what animal it was?

Mystery Animal

_____

_____

_____

_____

_____

_____

_____

_____

_____

_____

_____

_____

_____

_____

Name _____ **Date** _____

Look at the pictures. You are not told when the pictures were taken, but most likely, you can tell.

Write down two sentences about each picture. Tell during what season you think the picture was taken, and how you know.

Write a fifth sentence in which you explain which of the two seasons you like better and why.

Changing Seasons

1. _____

_____

_____

_____

2. _____

_____

_____

_____

3. _____

_____

_____

4. _____

_____

_____

_____

5. _____

_____

Name _____ Date _____

Two hard words to read are *wonderful* and *miserable*.

When something is *wonderful,* it is really great. When something is *miserable,* it is really awful.

Imagine you are teaching someone what these two hard words mean. Write two sentences (four in all) using each word.

Start two sentences with *I feel wonderful when . . .*

Start two sentences with *I feel miserable when . . .*

Winning Words

1. **I feel wonderful when** _____

_____

_____

2. _____

_____

_____

3. **I feel miserable when** _____

_____

_____

4. _____

_____

_____

Do you think someone could figure out what *wonderful* and *miserable* mean after reading your sentences? How?

_____

_____

A **fact** is a thing that has happened. A fact is true.

An **opinion** is what you think.

What's Your Opinion?

Count how many windows are in your classroom. Think about the number. Do you think there should be more or less? Why?

Write a paragraph in which your **first** sentence starts out like this:

It is a fact that my classroom has _____ *windows.*

Your **second** sentence starts out like this:

It is my opinion that . . .

Sentences **three** and **four** should tell why you think so. Give reasons why your opinion is a good one!

_____

_____

_____

_____

_____

_____

_____

_____

_____

_____

Name _____ **Date** _____

Write a dialogue between two children. In your dialogue, include at least one **fact** and one **opinion**.

When you write, pick your own names.

Remember to put a colon after the name of the person speaking.

A Friendly Chat

> *Example:*
>
> **Brian:** That dog is about the same size as a cat.
>
> **Melissa:** That's a fact.
>
> **Brian:** I think bigger dogs make better pets.
>
> **Melissa:** That's your opinion. I prefer small dogs!

_____

_____

_____

_____

_____

_____

_____

_____

_____

_____

Pick two classmates to read your dialogue to the class.

Name _____   **Date** _____

Is this story true? Write a paragraph in which you explain whether or not this story is factual, and why. Make sure you support your answer with **facts**!

Just a Monkey Tale?

> *I have a monkey that can fly. Some children ride the bus to school, but I go on my monkey's back. My monkey has purple hair and five legs. My monkey speaks English. My monkey eats bicycles.*

_____

_____

_____

_____

_____

_____

_____

_____

_____

_____

_____

_____

_____

_____

Name _____ Date _____

The king and queen are coming to your house for dinner! You get to serve them anything you want. In your **opinion**, what is the best meal you can give them? Pick what they will eat and drink. Think about why you think this is a good meal for a king and queen.

Start your paragraph by sharing what foods you will be serving the king and queen. Then, finish your paragraph by explaining why you chose these foods.

Preparing a Royal Feast

<u>When the king and queen come to dinner at my house,</u>

<u>I will serve them</u> _____

_____

_____

_____

_____

<u>I think this will be a good meal for a king and queen</u>

<u>because</u> _____

_____

_____

_____

_____

_____

Name _____ **Date** _____

Read this sentence:

I heard a noise, so I crawled under the bed.

I heard a noise is the **cause**. It is the reason **why** something happens.

I crawled under the bed is the **effect**. It is **what happens** because of the cause.

Finding Cause and Effect

Practice writing the part of the sentence that is the **cause**.

1. _____, so I drank three glasses of water.

2. When I _____, I found a dinosaur bone.

3. _____, so I put on mittens and a coat.

Practice writing the part of the sentence that is the **effect**.

1. I saw a zebra on the street, so _____.

2. When I went to the store, _____.

3. After my brother yelled at me, _____.

Now try one on your own! Make sure to show both **cause** and **effect**!

_____

_____

_____

_____

_____

_____

Name _____ **Date** _____

Think of three rules. Write them down.

Breaking the Rules

1. _____

_____

2. _____

_____

3. _____

_____

Now imagine that Silly Snake does not follow the rules. What effects does this have on Silly Snake? Write down what happens to Silly Snake when he doesn't follow the rules.

1. _____

_____

_____

_____

2. _____

_____

_____

_____

3. _____

_____

_____

_____

Farmer Mars and Farmer Venus both want to grow corn. Look at the pictures. Pick if you think Farmer Mars or Farmer Venus will grow more corn.

Give at least three reasons why one farmer's corn won't grow as well as the other farmer's corn.

A Tale of Two Farmers

Farmer Mars

Farmer Venus

1. _____

_____

_____

2. _____

_____

_____

3. _____

_____

_____

Name _____ **Date** _____

Look at the picture. Think about why the child is sad. What is the cause of his sadness? Then think about what will make the child feel better.

Why So Sad?

Write down one or two sentences about why the child is sad.

_____

_____

_____

_____

Write down one or two sentences about what might make the child feel better.

_____

_____

_____

_____

_____

Name _____   **Date** _____

Cereal for a Friend

Brock Moondancer has come to your house from another planet. He is going to eat breakfast with you. You tell him that you will be eating cereal. Brock Moondancer takes out a glass, fills it with water, and hits it with a fork!

You need to teach Brock Moondancer how to make a bowl of cereal for breakfast. Think of what you need. Think of all the steps. Write them down in order. Be sure to number your steps, too!

_____

_____

_____

_____

_____

_____

_____

_____

_____

_____

_____

_____

_____

_____

Name _____ **Date** _____

You have changed a lot. You can do a lot more things now than you could when you were smaller. Write something you could do at each age. Use complete sentences. You can write your sentences like this:

Look What I Can Do!

> *When I was one, I could* _____.
>
> **or**
>
> *I could* _____ *when I was one.*

1. _____

   _____

2. _____

   _____

3. _____

   _____

4. _____

   _____

5. _____

   _____

6. _____

   _____

7. _____

   _____

8. _____

   _____

Name _____ **Date** _____

When you write, these words help the reader know when things happened:

first, second, third, then, next, finally, after

Use at least three of these words when you make up a story about going into a **forest**, **jungle**, **lake**, or **ocean**.

> *Example:*
>
> *First, I went into a hot desert. Then I ran out of water, but I saw a camel. After the camel took me to an oasis, I filled up my water jug.*

You'll Never Believe This . . .

_____

_____

_____

_____

_____

_____

_____

_____

_____

_____

_____

_____

Name _____ **Date** _____

Look at the pictures. Think about what happened first, second, and last. Are the pictures in the correct order? Write a **1**, **2**, or **3** under each picture to show the correct order. Next, use these pictures to create a story and write a paragraph explaining what happened.

In What Order?

_____   _____   _____

_____

_____

_____

_____

_____

_____

_____

_____

Name _____ **Date** _____

Write down some jobs people do.

___<u>**astronaut**</u>___   _____

_____   _____

_____   _____

Who Am I?

Now write some hints about two of the jobs. Say some of the things the people do. After you write down your hints, write the words, "Who am I?"

Have your classmates read or listen to your clues. Could they figure out whom you were writing about?

Example:

Job: *astronaut*

Hints: *I go into space. I float in the air. I circle Earth. Who am I?*
(an astronaut)

Job: _____

Hints: _____

_____

_____

_____

Job: _____

Hints: _____

_____

_____

_____

_____

Name _____ **Date** _____

How many animal sound words can you think of?
Write them down.

If It Quacks Like a Duck . . .

_____ **quack** _____   _____

_____   _____

_____   _____

_____   _____

Even if you do not see the animal that quacks, you
may still infer that it is a duck. Pick four animal sounds
from the words you wrote down. Then write complete sentences in which you
explain what animal you expect to see and why.

Write your sentences like the examples below.

> _If I heard a quack, I might see a duck._
>
> **or**
>
> _I might see a duck if I heard a quack._

1. _____

   _____

   _____

2. _____

   _____

   _____

3. _____

   _____

   _____

4. _____

   _____

   _____

136

Name _____ **Date** _____

Most likely, you have never been in a deep, dark cave. Some scientists go into deep, dark caves for many days at a time. They might not see sunlight for many days. How do they know if it's daytime or nighttime?

Write down how you think the scientists live in such a dark environment. How do they eat? How do they know when to sleep? How do they see anything?

Did Anyone Bring a Flashlight?

_____

_____

_____

_____

_____

_____

_____

_____

_____

_____

_____

_____

_____

_____

_____

_____

Name _____ **Date** _____

You are not told what is going to happen next, but you can come up with a good idea.

Write down a sentence or two in which you describe the scene. Then tell what is going to happen next.

Use your imagination when you write your sentences for these pictures!

What Happens Next?

_____
_____
_____
_____
_____
_____
_____
_____

_____
_____
_____
_____
_____
_____
_____
_____

Name _____ **Date** _____

When people cook, they often use a recipe. The recipe may tell them how many eggs to use or how long the cooking time is.

Make up a new food. Your food can have a wild or silly name if you want. Write down a recipe for your new food. Include ingredients, baking temperature, and cooking time.

Building a Recipe

_____
(name of your new food)

Ingredients:

_____   _____

_____   _____

_____   _____

_____   _____

Baking Temperature: _____

Baking Time: _____

Now **predict** who will eat it and what it will taste like.

_____

_____

_____

_____

_____

Name _____ **Date** _____

Imagine that you are given two wishes. You can wish for anything you want. Your wishes can be big or small.

Write a paragraph about your wishes. Start it like this:

If I were given two wishes, my first wish would . . .

Then tell what changes might occur or what might happen because of your wish.

My Two Wishes

_____

_____

_____

_____

_____

_____

_____

_____

_____

_____

_____

_____

Common Core State Standards Correlations

Each activity in *Instant Reading Comprehension Practice* meets one or more of the following Common Core State Standards (© Copyright 2010. National Governors Association Center for Best Practices and Council of Chief State School Officers. All rights reserved.). For more information about the Common Core State Standards, go to *http://www.corestandards.org* or visit *http://www.teachercreated.com/standards*.

Reading: Literature	
Key Ideas and Details	**Pages**
ELA.RL.2.1 Ask and answer such questions as *who, what, where, when, why*, and *how* to demonstrate understanding of key details in a text.	6–17, 19, 20, 21–35, 55–65, 66–80, 81–95, 96–110
ELA.RL.2.2 Recount stories, including fables and folktales from diverse cultures, and determine their central message, lesson, or moral.	6–17, 19, 20
ELA.RL.2.3 Describe how characters in a story respond to major events and challenges.	96–110
Integration of Knowledge and Ideas	**Pages**
ELA.RL.2.7 Use information gained from the illustrations and words in a print or digital text to demonstrate understanding of its characters, setting, or plot.	6–17, 19, 20, 21–35, 36–50, 55–65, 66–80, 81–95, 96–110
Range of Reading and Level of Text Complexity	**Pages**
ELA.RL.2.10 By the end of the year, read and comprehend literature, including stories and poetry, in the grades 2–3 text complexity band proficiently, with scaffolding as needed at the high end of the range.	6–17, 19, 20, 21–35, 36–50, 55–65, 66–80, 81–95, 96–110

Reading: Informational Text	
Key Ideas and Details	**Pages**
ELA.RI.2.1 Ask and answer such questions as *who, what, where, when, why*, and *how* to demonstrate understanding of key details in a text.	6, 8–10, 13, 15–18
ELA.RI.2.2 Identify the main topic of a multiparagraph text as well as the focus of specific paragraphs within the text.	6, 8–10, 13, 15–18
Craft and Structure	**Pages**
ELA.RI.2.4 Determine the meaning of words and phrases in a text relevant to a *grade 2 topic or subject area*.	6, 8–10, 13, 15–18, 44, 46, 51–54
ELA.RI.2.6 Identify the main purpose of a text, including what the author wants to answer, explain, or describe.	6, 8–10, 13, 15–18, 51–54
Range of Reading and Level of Text Complexity	**Pages**
ELA.RI.2.10 By the end of year, read and comprehend informational texts, including history/social studies, science, and technical texts, in the grades 2–3 text complexity band proficiently, with scaffolding as needed at the high end of the range.	6, 8–10, 13, 15–18, 44, 46, 51–54

Reading: Foundational Skills

Phonics and Word Recognition	Pages
ELA.RF.2.3 Know and apply grade-level phonics and word analysis skills in decoding words.	6–20, 21–35, 36–50, 51–54, 55–65, 66–80, 81–95, 96–110
ELA.RF.2.3.A Distinguish long and short vowels when reading regularly spelled one-syllable words.	6–20, 21–35, 36–50, 51–54, 55–65, 66–80, 81–95, 96–110
ELA.RF.2.3.B Know spelling-sound correspondences for additional common vowel teams.	6–20, 21–35, 36–50, 51–54, 55–65, 66–80, 81–95, 96–110
ELA.RF.2.3.C Decode regularly spelled two-syllable words with long vowels.	6–20, 21–35, 36–50, 51–54, 55–65, 66–80, 81–95, 96–110
ELA.RF.2.3.D Decode words with common prefixes and suffixes.	6–20, 21–35, 36–50, 51–54, 55–65, 81–95, 96–110

Fluency	Pages
ELA.RF.2.4 Read with sufficient accuracy and fluency to support comprehension.	6–20, 21–35, 36–50, 51–54, 55–65, 66–80, 81–95, 96–110
ELA.RF.2.4.A Read grade-level text with purpose and understanding.	6–20, 21–35, 36–50, 51–54, 55–65, 66–80, 81–95, 96–110
ELA.RF.2.4.C Use context to confirm or self-correct word recognition and understanding, rereading as necessary.	6–20, 21–35, 36–50, 51–54, 55–65, 66–80, 81–95, 96–110

Writing

Text Type and Purposes	Pages
ELA.W.2.1 Write opinion pieces in which they introduce the topic or book they are writing about, state an opinion, supply reasons that support the opinion, use linking words (e.g., *because*, *and*, *also*) to connect opinion and reasons, and provide a concluding statement or section.	111, 121, 123–127, 129, 134, 137, 138
ELA.W.2.2 Write informative/explanatory texts in which they introduce a topic, use facts and definitions to develop points, and provide a concluding statement or section.	111, 112, 115–118, 120, 121, 124, 127, 135, 139
ELA.W.2.3 Write narratives in which they recount a well-elaborated event or short sequence of events, include details to describe actions, thoughts, and feelings, use temporal words to signal event order, and provide a sense of closure.	113, 114, 117–119, 122, 124, 127, 128, 130–133, 136, 138, 140

Production and Distribution of Writing	Pages
ELA.W.2.5 With guidance and support from adults and peers, focus on a topic and strengthen writing as needed by revising and editing.	116, 119, 120
ELA.W.2.6 With guidance and support from adults, use a variety of digital tools to produce and publish writing, including in collaboration with peers.	117

Research to Build and Present Knowledge	Pages
ELA.W.2.8 Recall information from experiences or gather information from provided sources to answer a question.	116, 117, 119–122, 131, 136, 137

Answer Key

Finding Main Ideas
Page 6
Snowy Surprise: A
Dizzy Days: A
Page 7
A Hole in One: C
Lost Friend: B
Page 8
Big Cats: B
Shoe Business: C
Page 9
Speedy Sneezys: A
Fright Night!: B
Page 10
Danger Drop: C
The Human Spider: C
Page 11
Four-Legged Friend: B
Race to the Finish: A
Page 12
A Fish Tale: C
First-Day Fashion: B
Page 13
The Picky Parrot: B
Across the Ice: B
Page 14
Jumping for Joy: C
A Star Is Born: A
Page 15
What a Knight!: A
A Huge Heart: C
Page 16
Birthday Surprise: A
Big Bones: B
Page 17
Nature's Medicine: A
Goodbye, Green: C
Page 18
Baby Talk: B
A Full Deck: B
Page 19
Doggy Decisions: C
The Boy Who Could
   (Almost) Fly: A
Page 20
A Surprise Visitor: A
The Riddle: C

Noting Details
Page 21
Summer Fun: B
Feeding Frenzy: C
Page 22
Everybody Dance!: B
Loud Laundry: A
Page 23
Fishing with Dad: B
A Rough Start: A
Page 24
Rebecca and the Bear: C
Animal Artist: B
Page 25
Pants Problem: A
Up to Date: C
Page 26
Meeting Patch: C
No More Fears: C
Page 27
Treasure in the Park: A
Wheels and Meals: B
Page 28
Puppy Pals: A
Camp Living Room: C
Page 29
Quackers and Water: A
Going, Going, Gone: C
Page 30
Say, "Cheese!": B
Flag Gab: A
Page 31
Smiles After the Storm: B
Pony Promises: C
Page 32
The Lonely Walk: B
Bookworm: A
Page 33
A Surprising Discovery: C
Being Crafty: B
Page 34
Sack Race: A
Laundry Day: B
Page 35
Olympic Dreams: C
Lots-o-Legs: A

Using Context Clues
Page 36
Riding High: C
A Summer Treat: C
Page 37
Cheap Seats: B
Missed Call: A
Page 38
A Happy Helper: A
Breakfast Time!: B
Page 39
A New Type
   of Sandwich: C
Who's Right?: B
Page 40
Shake, Rattle, and Roll: A
Grocery-Store Guy: A
Page 41
Early Explorers: B
A Long Walk Home: B
Page 42
Gold in the Ground: C
Off Her Feet: C
Page 43
Surrounded by Stripes: B
Two Toys in One: A
Page 44
Map Reading: B
Practicing for the Game: C
Page 45
Don't Be a Litterbug: A
Best Dressed: A
Page 46
Garden Fresh: C
Little Ones: B
Page 47
Last Man Standing: B
Young Authors: C
Page 48
What's for Dinner?: A
Holiday Feast: B
Page 49
Give Dad a Hand: C
Old News: A
Page 50
Lunch Break: A
Out with the Old: C

Identifying Facts and Opinions
Page 51
Check a Calendar: Fact
Funday Monday: Opinion
May I Borrow
   Those?: Opinion
Fine Print: Fact
Dinner Time: Opinion
Make New
   Friends: Opinion
Big Dog, Little Dog: Fact
The Cat's Meow: Opinion
Page 52
Scary Seas: Opinion
Mental Math: Fact
Ask Picasso: Fact
Storytellers: Opinion
That's a Big Omelet!: Fact
Junior Pilot: Opinion
Pleasant Plants: Fact
Road Trip!: Opinion
Page 53
Zoo Babies: B
No-Fly Zone: B
Corny Comparison: A
Math Facts: A
It's Tricky: A
No Bib, No Service: A
Colors of the World: B
Clock Talk: B
Page 54
Eye Caramba!: B
Tomato Time: A
Healthy Habits: A
Paper Views: B
It's Black and White: B
Hip to Be Square: A
A Dog's Worst Friend: A
A Pickle of a Problem: A

Finding Cause and Effect

Page 55
Ouch!: B
Fourth of July: B
BBQ Smile: A
Pucker Up!: A
Scooter Scotty: B

Page 56
First Things First: B
Money Toss: B
Soup Night: A
Just What I Wanted!: B
Safe Drivers: A

Page 57
A Day at the Park: B
Storm Watch: A
Make a Wish: A
Always Look Both Ways: A
Buried Bones: B

Page 58
All Tripped Up: C
Morning Appetite: B

Page 59
Unprepared: A
Feeling Shy: C

Page 60
Looking Up: A
A Friendly Contest: C

Page 61
Oh, Brother!: B
Keeping It Cool: B

Page 62
Take Me Out to the Ballgame: A
Cammy the Camel: B

Page 63
Too Much Salt!: C
Falling Leaves: C

Page 64
Worst Flight Ever: A
Little Bee, Big Buzz: C

Page 65
Extra Recess: B
Now Where Was I?: A

Sequencing

Page 66
Spilled Milk: A
Muddy Surprise: C

Page 67
Cleaning My Room: C
Not a Great Plan: B

Page 68
New Faces: B
Milky Mess: A

Page 69
Juice Party: A
Baby on the Move: C

Page 70
Learning the Rules: A
Safety First: B

Page 71
Race in the Park: B
Fear Factor: C

Page 72
Pool Party: B
Swimming Lessons: A

Page 73
Saved by the Socks: C
Smells Like Breakfast: B

Page 74
Mark's New Look: A
A Sight for Sore Eyes: C

Page 75
Dad to the Rescue: C
Farm Friends: A

Page 76
Our Own Pumpkin Patch: A
Evan's Clean Teeth: C

Page 77
Is It Magic?: B
Too Cold!: B

Page 78
A Net Full of Water: C
Playful Puppy: A

Page 79
Mail from a Friend: A
Building Castles: B

Page 80
Junior Banker: C
Tales of Adventure: B

Making Inferences

Page 81
Terry's Busy Day: A
First Day of Practice: C

Page 82
Cold Tub: B
A Stinky Cat?: B

Page 83
Band Practice: C
Beat the Heat: A

Page 84
No Ordinary Job: C
A Great Day in Mudville: B

Page 85
Practice Makes Perfect: A
Celebration Day: B

Page 86
Lincoln's Books: C
Late-Night Party: A

Page 87
Slow Down!: A
Lights Out: B

Page 88
Some Assembly Required: C
No, Thanks: A

Page 89
Snow Day: C
It's Not a Dog: B

Page 90
Stinky Cheese: C
A Stormy Night: A

Page 91
Too Many Questions: A
Hearts: C

Page 92
A Well-Earned Reward: B
Two Cold Poles: B

Page 93
The Purple Top: C
Bus Adventure: B

Page 94
Tickets and Smiles: A
Walking Safely: B

Page 95
The Perfect Food: A
The Girl Who Could See Through Walls: C

Predicting Outcomes

Page 96
Bad Habits: A
Something Different: C

Page 97
A Trip to Star Town: B
Mom Knows Best: B

Page 98
Shirt Shopping: A
Spring Forward: C

Page 99
Too Hot to Play: B
Will It Be Windy?: A

Page 100
Party in the Rain: C
Wet Paint: C

Page 101
Follow the Recipe: B
A Generous Gift: A

Page 102
Feeling Crabby: B
Simple Signals: C

Page 103
Direct Hit!: A
Grandma's Gifts: B

Page 104
Green Thumb: C
Over the Curb: B

Page 105
Walk to the Top: A
Without a Bib: A

Page 106
Cookie Milk: C
Bug Boy: B

Page 107
Good Listener: B
Capital Kids: C

Page 108
Big-Girl Bike: C
Signs: A

Page 109
Time for a Change: C
Night Reader: B

Page 110
Great Burgers: A
Big Baby: A